BRIGITTE BRÜGGEMANN

By keeping to her upfront, intended narrative of illustrating process and the events leading to her artist-self being free in the world, Brigitte Brüggemann manages to avoid the cinematic temptations of over-colorizing her life with the very real explanation of how her roles as a wife and mother had to be undone in order to find herself.

—**David Sawyer**, artist

Near the end of that devastating war, in a city in ruins, a little girl wanders into a bombed-out building and discovers a bunch of Mickey Mouse pins attached to a wire. Her mother is horrified that it might be a booby trap. Brigitte writes of gleaning a farmer's field for potatoes as an American fighter pilot swoops down strafing the earth, causing her with her mother and sisters to flee into the forest. Now she is in New Mexico, an accomplished abstract artist of imaginative form and brilliant color. Her work hangs in museums and in people's homes throughout the world.

—**Joseph Bottone**, poet

GROWING WINGS
A STORY OF BECOMING

Aufstieg

BRIGITTE BRÜGGEMANN

Copyright © 2021 Brigitte Brüggemann.

All rights reserved. No part of this book may be used or reproduced by any means, graphic, electronic, or mechanical, including photocopying, recording, taping or by any information storage retrieval system without the written permission of the author except in the case of brief quotations embodied in critical articles and reviews.

This book is a work of non-fiction. Unless otherwise noted, the author and the publisher make no explicit guarantees as to the accuracy of the information contained in this book and in some cases, names of people and places have been altered to protect their privacy.

Archway Publishing books may be ordered through booksellers or by contacting:

Archway Publishing
1663 Liberty Drive
Bloomington, IN 47403
www.archwaypublishing.com
844-669-3957

For sale with the author at www.brigittebruggemann.com

cover image title "Aufstieg"

Because of the dynamic nature of the Internet, any web addresses or links contained in this book may have changed since publication and may no longer be valid. The views expressed in this work are solely those of the author and do not necessarily reflect the views of the publisher, and the publisher hereby disclaims any responsibility for them.

Cover and Interior Image Credit: Brigitte Brüggemann

ISBN: 978-1-6657-0950-7 (sc)
ISBN: 978-1-6657-0949-1 (hc)

Library of Congress Control Number: 2021914083

Print information available on the last page.

Archway Publishing rev. date: 11/15/2021

CONTENTS

PART 1: WAR

CHAPTER 1   My Story Begins Before I Was Born 3

CHAPTER 2   Images of War 5

CHAPTER 3   My Brother is American 8

CHAPTER 4   Survival 9

CHAPTER 5   Postwar Life 11

CHAPTER 6   No Deal in the Tramway—1948 13

CHAPTER 7   Children of War 14

CHAPTER 8   Going to the Races 19

CHAPTER 9   Roller Coaster 24

CHAPTER 10 Christmas 26

CHAPTER 11 Hard Times—First Calling 30

CHAPTER 12 Lost in the Forest 35

PART 2: FINDING MY PATH

CHAPTER 13 Soul Searching 39

CHAPTER 14 Plan B—1962 Stuttgart 43

CHAPTER 15 Leaving the Nest—Paris 1964 45

CHAPTER 16 Finding a Landing Place 47

CHAPTER 17 Walkabout 52

CHAPTER 18 Limbo Rock 55

CHAPTER 19 Losing Myself for a While 57

CHAPTER 20 Getting Closer: Memphis Academy of Art—1975 58

CHAPTER 21 Art Has Me Now—Colorado 62

CHAPTER 22　The Art of Becoming 64

CHAPTER 23　Undergraduate Years 66

CHAPTER 24　Signs and Wonders 74

CHAPTER 25　Trust 76

CHAPTER 26　Teaching: Las Vegas, NM—1990 78

CHAPTER 27　Finding my Place—Two Years Later 82

CHAPTER 28　Painter of Light 86

CHAPTER 29　The Kiss of the Hummingbird 88

CHAPTER 30　Building a Painter's Dream 90

PART 3: MAKING IT WORK

CHAPTER 31　Painting Is the Work 99

CHAPTER 32　Stretching my Wings 100

CHAPTER 33　Into the Unknown 102

CHAPTER 34　Painting is meditation 105

CHAPTER 35　The Business of Art 108

CHAPTER 36　The Power of Paint and Color 111

CHAPTER 37　The Process of Painting 115

PART 4: OTHER PLACES AND THINGS

A wound is the place where
the light enters you.

—Rumi

PREFACE

A long road traveled left dust on my feet. With memories of childhood trauma brushed aside but not forgotten, my quest for independence combined with my curiosity for the unfamiliar and new, my passion for art and creative living, along with my travels to distant places all became a story asking to be told.

At seventy-something, it was time for me to sort through my journals and memories to create, not with paint but with words, a picture of a life lived with intention, with curiosity for the unfamiliar, overcoming obstacles and going with the flow like a river finding its way to the ocean. The story is also about finding my spiritual path and purpose, getting lost in detours at times with doubts and heartbreaks, but finding signposts here and there to show the way.

With my paintings, I try to bring light into people's living rooms. With my stories, I want to show how much is possible in spite of what one might perceive as impossible dreams. Art washed the dust off my feet.

This book is about honoring the gifts given: follow that inner voice, take risks, go into the unknown, walk the unfamiliar path. Help will meet you on the way.

Feel the Wings You Have Grown

Searching the distance between the stars
I have grown wings.
Traveling through darkness in my sleep,
fearless,
to find what I have lost long ago.
I do not remember what I am looking for,
but
I know it is for me to find
slicing through darkness,
a feathered wing soft and strong
caressing me with love
holding me,
guiding me to find what I have lost
long ago.
Here on earth,
the sun still warm on my back,
my hands digging in the soil,
I plant new hope:
two lips
to sing the first song of new life
after winter has gone.

New Mexico

Cool morning—heartbeat—I listen.
I hear the sound of water in the pond,
birdsong in the tree,
the rustle of aspen leaves.
I see tall grass catching the morning sun,
the day is an empty space in front of me,
a white canvas
asking to be filled with marks.
My mind wants to fill the canvas,
my heart says be still and listen.
This is all there is
Is this not enough for you?
Stop seeking.

My garden has grown with the help of the devas. Birds wake me up with their morning song. A robin is perched on top of a pine tree outside my bedroom window as if in prayer, facing the rising sun in the east. I hear the river rushing by; I see the sparkling silver ribbon between the trees. Like the little bird on top of the tree, I am filled with gratitude for the guidance and love I have received.

The road I traveled has been rocky, with many turns and detours, many serendipitous events leading and guiding me from a difficult childhood in post-war Germany, living in foreign countries, starting over many times, and finding this place in New Mexico by a river where I am living a painter's dream.

House with Wings and Wheels, watercolor

To the River triptych, pastel

The river, my teacher, has been a constant companion. I sit by it, bring to it my joys and woes. I watch the raging waters at times, when uprooted trees come rushing by—chaos after a storm, the red, violent river muddy. I step aside, watch the force of nature with awe. Other times, I watch the calm, soothing flow, leaves floating in the eddy going round and round until suddenly they are pulled by an invisible force into the mainstream, on their way to the ocean.

PART ONE
W A R

CHAPTER 1

MY STORY BEGINS BEFORE I WAS BORN

It was wartime in Germany. Hitler's soldiers had marched into Austria, invaded Czechoslovakia, France, Belgium, Holland, Norway, Poland and Russia, as well as fighting battles in Africa. Hitler's madness—and that of the people believing in *the Führer*—had set our world on fire.

Stuttgart, Germany: my mother was pregnant with her third child, she was not well. Besides her worries about bringing another child into a world at war, she needed surgery for various health issues. The doctor told her she could lose the child, and maybe, she thought, in wartime, that would be for the best.

In a dream, a bright being appeared to her: "You will carry this child; it will bring you joy."

We survived the surgery. I was born in the middle of that terrible war. I first saw the light August 23, 1942—the same day the German Sixth Army reached the outskirts of Stalingrad. It was a dark time, the beginning of the end for the Third Reich.

During the last two years of the war, 1943 through 1945. The fighting came very close, came into the "Fatherland" with bombings, night raids, blackouts, and screeching sirens. People rushed to basements and bomb shelters with coats thrown hastily over nightclothes. Mothers carried a suitcase with some necessities in one hand and their baby in the other arm. Small children clutched their mother's skirts. Muffled cries and whispered prayers filled the crowded, stifling darkness of the shelters, with the roaring sound of bombers above. "Christmas trees," target indicator flares, were falling from the sky like fireworks, illuminating the night sky and the targets for the bombs. Anti-aircraft rockets were shooting up from the hills around the city. Explosions, whole city blocks were on fire—devastation, death, fear, and hopelessness. By the end of the war, 60 percent of Stuttgart, my hometown, was in ruins. The fierce bombing had caused firestorms that sucked the oxygen from the air. People were trapped in shelters or suffocated trying to flee to nowhere. Death was a constant presence, leaving deep scars on people's bodies, minds, and spirits.

Those very early years of my life have affected my psyche. Memories pushed into the unconscious are deeply buried in my soul, forever seeking peace and light. My earliest conscious memories are of fire and ruins for a playground.

Today, more than seven decades later, in New Mexico, I sit in the sun outside my house overlooking the Pecos River, a silver bracelet rushing to the ocean, ever-moving, ever-changing, always new. The river has been my teacher for many years now: nothing stays the same. Water knows no scars. It goes around obstacles, goes around the rocks in its path, without pain— maybe a little whitewater, but then it flows on to the ocean. The path is the destiny. I have encountered many rocks in my path. While going around them might have been wiser, often that was not my best choice. I have wasted much energy fighting obstacles, climbing up and down mountains—emotional and real ones—while growing my wings. At times I was the mountain myself, standing in my own way, holding on to learned patterns and traditional roles that did not serve me. My intention became clearer as I grew into adulthood: to follow my bliss, to seek a lightness of being

My passion is for art.

My mission is to manifest joyful and uplifting images.

My tools are brush and paint, pen and paper.

My voice is to bring healing for myself in the process of painting and to manifest uplifting energy into imagery for those who choose to live with and see my work.

A quote from the Indian mystic Osho, my spiritual teacher, may take this to the extreme, but I share that spirit:

> Life can only be lived dangerously—there is no other way to live it. It is through danger, taking risks, go into the unknown and the unfamiliar one can find maturity and growth. My path was and still is to be adventurous, always ready to risk the known for the unknown. And once one has tasted the joys of freedom and fearlessness one never repents because then one knows what it means to live at the optimum. Then one knows to burn your life's torch from both ends together. And even a single moment of that intensity is more gratifying than the whole eternity of mediocre living.

CHAPTER 2

IMAGES OF WAR

My earliest memories are mixed with the stories my mother told many times. She spoke without emotion, detached, focused on a distant point as if she could see those images. Even years after the war, when a plane flew low overhead, she would duck in fear with terror in her eyes. Her words reverberated in me as if I had been there—and I had been.

When I was in my forties, I had a reoccurring lucid dream: I am a small child sitting in the dark on a pile of something lumpy, unstable, uncomfortable. I feel the presence of others; I am not alone in the darkness. In the flickering light in front of me, I see the frame of a small square basement window with iron bars forming a cross. The source for the flickering light is fire—the outside world is on fire.

During a visit with my older sister, we had a conversation about dreams. I told her about this recurring dream. She sat up straight, looked at me with eyes wide open, and cried out, "But that was real! You remember in your dream what happened." She explained that we all had sat in the root cellar on a pile of potatoes while the village was burning. Our father was there with us three children. My sister could not remember more details, so I asked my mother to tell me the whole story.

In 1944 and 1945, the battles of the war had come into Germany with Allied bombings and ground combat. We had been evacuated from the city to a farming village in the southwest of Germany "for the safety of women and children." We lived in a farmhouse annex on the village square. In front of our small house was a fountain running with fresh water.

The Allied forces had divided up German territory for combat, for liberation from the Nazi terror: the British in the north, the Russians in the east, and the French and Americans in the south and west towards Stuttgart, Frankfurt, and Munich.

Retreating German soldiers were hiding in the forest near Saugart, our village, not far from Stuttgart, the capital of the region. It was a tense time, filled with fear and uncertainty. One night, from the upstairs bedroom window, Mother could see German soldiers, with guns over their shoulders, sneaking to the village fountain. They carried their marching boots and tiptoed in their socks so they wouldn't make any noise. After filling their helmets with water, they quietly retreated into the forest.

One sunny summer day, decades later, in my garden in New Mexico, I was coming around the corner of my house and froze in my steps. There was a large snake, about five feet long, peacefully catching the drips from the garden spigot with her long-forked tongue. I listened for the warning sound of a rattlesnake, but there was none. It was a bull snake. I could safely watch her drinking from the fountain. I flashed back to that wartime story, the image of soldiers coming to the fountain to fetch water and then silently retreating, as did the snake. I watched as she slithered through the grass and disappeared—two images, one of war and one of peace.

But I return to my mother and her story of why our village was burning. One day, a German motorcycle with a sidecar marked as a Red Cross vehicle ambushed a French ambulance unit, killing two French nurses. An eye for an eye, the French cried out, revenge! In the center of the village, they ambushed a retreating German army truck carrying soldiers standing shoulder to shoulder on the open flatbed. The French, with a machine gun, mowed the soldiers down like wheat in a field, and set the village on fire.

This is where my dream comes in: We children and our father hid in the cellar. My mother was upstairs doing the best she could to prevent our house from burning. My father, a civilian, was with us because he was never enlisted in the army; neither was he a member of the Nazi party. He got in trouble for his resistance to become a member. When a Nazi came to our apartment in the city one day to recruit him for the party, father refused and, in his frustration, pushed the man down the stairs. The next day, the SS came to take Father away to send him to the front. Father was a sought-after mechanic, some of the local influential German officers were his clients. One of Dad's clients needed a repair for his car. Father came home again the next day with his hair shaved like a soldier's, back from the recruitment barracks, saved from being sent to the front, he was "more important to the war effort at home."

In the chaos during the end of the war, those privileges did not work for him anymore, and he was with us in the countryside to avoid being taken prisoner of war. With the village in flames, we hid in the basement. Upstairs, a Moroccan soldier serving with the French army had come into the house. He forced my mother to go up the stairs with a gun to her back. "*Komm mit*, Marie," he said. As they moved up the stairs, my mother said in her schoolgirl French, "*Je suis malade. J'ai syphilis.*" It was a lie, but it saved her from being raped and possibly killed. The soldier left after eating a raw onion from the kitchen like it was an apple and taking the little coin banks from our bedroom. They were shaped like little houses in the style of Black Forest chalets, with little trees, rocks on the roof, balconies, and flower boxes on the windows.

Guardian Spirit, pastel

CHAPTER 3

MY BROTHER IS AMERICAN

The American troops had come into the village searching for weapons and looking for any signs of resistance—German soldiers or any man in hiding. My father had come from the heavily bombed city to stay with us for safety and had parked his car in front of the house. He removed the distributor cap so the vehicle could not be started and had hidden the part in the house in a chimney.

A parked car with a license plate from the city in a farming village during wartime was suspicious, and its presence resulted in a search of our house. The part was discovered. Father was accused of resistance and was taken away to a prisoner of war camp nearby.

Mother, the warrior-woman she was, decided against all odds to try to rescue him. She walked miles to the Allied American camp, asking to speak with the commanding officer. "He has not done anything wrong!" she said. "He never was a soldier!" And then she exclaimed, "My brother is an American!" (Her brother had emigrated to the States in the late twenties.)

Miraculously, the Americans released my father.

It was the end of World War Two. Germany was destined to surrender to the Allies, but fierce last-ditch fighting was still going on in the forests and meadows around our small village. Many soldiers saw the end of the war coming. They got rid of their weapons and uniforms, defected or went into hiding somewhere, waiting for the right moment to surrender to the Americans. Others held on to the illusion that the Führer's "secret weapon" would change the outcome of the war. The Nazi Werewolf movement was engaged in fighting the Allies and any German defectors or collaborators with the enemy. In the last days of the war, tragic executions happened between Hitler's hardline believers and those wanting to surrender.

CHAPTER 4

SURVIVAL

Food was sparse. Farmer Maier traded milk and eggs with us for passport pictures for the ID cards required to pass the checkpoints when travel from one village to the next was needed. Mutti converted her fine Leica camera into an enlarger/projector for developing the negatives, using a closet as a darkroom and some photographic paper she had saved from her pre-war hobby. She had been an aspiring photographer as a young woman.

Her sewing skills became another source of barter for food. She made alterations to transform farmer Maier's rumpled coats and suits into a "first suit" for his teenage son who was preparing for the Christian ritual of Confirmation.

Important food items for us young children—eggs, milk, and butter—could be traded for from farmers, the cows and chickens providing, but we needed other sustenance like potatoes as well as flour to make bread. In the search for food, we all went gathering, gleaning the fields after the potato harvest. With our hands we dug into the soil to find the "forgotten fruit" in the earth—*Kartoffeln*, *pomme de terre* (apple of the earth). For me, toddling along, the field was a sandbox to play in. It was treasure hunt! We gathered wheat that had fallen by the wayside after the harvest machines had gone through, collecting the seed heads one by one for a bit of flour. Another make-believe play was to take our doll carriage into the forest and fill it with the nuts that had fallen from the beech trees. The tiny, shiny, delicious brown triangular beechnuts were rich in oil and nutrients. They were pressed for precious oil at the mill.

On one clear day, Mom put us three girls on her "iron horse"—her bicycle—and off we went to find some potatoes. My oldest sister, who was about seven years old, was riding on the bicycle seat. My five-year-old sister was on the luggage rack, and I, the youngest and smallest, just two years old, sat in the basket attached to the handlebar. Mom pushed the heavily loaded bike along a gravelly dirt path, taking us out of the village to a potato field at the edge of a forest. The path was lined by an irrigation ditch overgrown with stinging nettle weeds.

Fighting was still going on, and it was daring—even reckless—to go out. Suddenly, a fighter plane was overhead. Mutti threw us all, with the bike, into the ditch. The stinging nettle weeds gave us some cover. Radatdatdatdatdaa!

The pilot was looking down on us from his cockpit. Bullets hit the ground in a row on one side of us, throwing up fountains of black soil and rocks, but missing us. It was like a scene in a war movie, it was a real-life scene in a war. We did not even feel the sting of the nettles. With screaming motors, the plane roared on over the forest nearby. We scrambled out of the ditch. Mutti carried me as she and my sisters ran into the forest for cover. By the time the plane came back for us, we had reached the forest—saved, to live. I wonder today, how the pilot was justifying his actions to his conscience.

1944, mother and her 3 girls

Many years later, during a divination practice, I asked about my spiritual contract in this life—What am I to accomplish and learn in this life? I received a message in a code of images: black dots like bullet holes in a row. Was this memory, escaping death, meant to show me the preciousness of every moment in life, to do the soul's work but also the artist's work?

CHAPTER 5

POSTWAR LIFE

After the war ended, people started to clear the rubble, find a way to live in the ruins, and rebuild. Bricks from crumbled walls and all material that could be reused were cleaned and used for patching-up jobs. Much of this cleaning-up was done by the women—the *Trümmer-Frauen* (rubble women), doing this hard work because so many men had not returned from the war. Many houses were unstable and had to be taken down completely. All rubble was piled up in the middle of the street, to be carted off by the truckloads later, sometimes years later.

Food was rationed. People had to stand in line for hours at times, taking turns between family members. Often, when one finally got to the counter in the grocery store, there was nothing left. The old Reichsmark currency was worthless, and everyone had to start with very few Deutsche Mark.

Wikipedia:

Quote: The merchants, hoping for new money, hoarded their wares, with a population badly in need. The American cigarettes played the role of money so well, that an actual 'cigarette currency' was spoken of. Coffee and tea from allied soldiers were also a favored medium of exchange. The black market also boomed, delivering food, clothing and all necessities for a high price. In many major cities, like Frankfurt or Munich, was the market out in the open, attempts at its suppression failed. The rations were insufficient, people hungered and froze, and especially the old and children died. A new currency, the Deutsche Mark (DM), was created and the Reichsmark, Renten-mark and Militär-mark lost their validity; so, did most of the coins. Every single person received a sum of 60 Deutsche Mark (40 DM immediately, the rest two months later). Employers received 60 DM per employee" Unquote (at the time that would have been about $15)"

The days were filled with struggles for food and shelter. Many people had lost their homes. The local population was flooded with refugees arriving from the east, fleeing westward toward the American zone in fear of the fierce Russian army. Thousands had to be accommodated. Any "available" room was assigned to a refugee family. The five members of our family shared our apartment of three rooms with a refugee family of four from Dresden.

At mealtimes, my mother would serve each of us as we sat around the table, Father first, then her three children. Often there was nothing left for Mutti to serve herself. When we asked, "what about you?"

she would say, "Oh, I already ate in the kitchen." As small as I was, I never believed her and silently questioned why my father did not look after her as he should have. When I look at a photograph that was taken at that time, it is clear that I was right.

"You may say I'm a dreamer,"[1]

Brigitte and her mom, 1945

There was an antiaircraft station and bunker at the edge of town, containing guns, ammunition and rockets. The Allies ordered that it should be blown up or filled in. Because it was close to town, an explosion could have caused more damage to buildings nearby still standing. Had we not had enough explosions? The bunker was filled in, and a "mountain," about five hundred meters high, was created over it with truckloads and truckloads of rubble that had been piled up in the streets of the city. We called the rubble mountain Monte Scherbelino—a Mountain of Shards.

A road led to the top, which in time became a place of worship and a war memorial overlooking the city. For many years after, we went to Easter sunrise service there, the annual celebration of rebirth. The congregation gathered by a cross made from burned timbers, surrounded by broken sculptures, columns, and parts of buildings, witnesses to the madness we had survived.

---

[1] From the song "Imagine"—lyrics by John Lennon

CHAPTER 6

NO DEAL IN THE TRAMWAY—1948

Streetcars were running again; the tracks had been repaired and most of the rubble cleared. Tickets for the ride were costly, and it was a treat for us to take the yellow tram #9 from our house to the center of the city and back. We would walk one way to where we had to go, sometimes for miles. For the return trip on the streetcar, we had saved up the fare. This, for me as a small child, was a real adventure.

On one of those trips, my mother and I sat in what was my favorite seat right by the door. Instead of the usual bench for two people facing the opposite bench for two, there was only one seat near the entrance for the elderly and disabled with one seat opposite, the two passengers facing each other. I loved that seat! It was "intimate" with a little tray table between the seats. In my imagination, someone could eat lunch or have a cup of tea there.

One day, on one of the stops, an older man got onboard. Because I had been taught to give up my seat for older people, I stood up and held on to my mother's shoulder. The man sat down opposite my mother. He looked foreign. He spoke with an accent when he thanked me for giving up my seat for him. He looked gray, his coat was gray and rumpled; his face was gray with a two-day growth of gray stubble

He took a long calculating look at me and then looked at my mother. "Do you have other children?" he asked. She crunched her shoulder up slightly and, with hesitation, said, "Yes, I have two more girls." He nodded and slowly pulled out a big wad of money. He put it on the little tray table and said, "Then you would not miss this one? I buy her from you. Things will be easier for you then." My mother immediately stood up from her seat, grabbed my hand and, without a word, left the tram at the next stop. Mutti looked back over her shoulder to make sure the man was not following us. She held my hand as we walked the rest of the way home.

CHAPTER 7

CHILDREN OF WAR

Stuttgart had been hard hit; the street we lived on, Rosenberg Strasse, was mostly ruined. The target for the bombs that hit our neighborhood was the original Bosch manufacturing plant nearby that had been ordered by the German Military Command to manufacture equipment for the war effort, making it a major target. Also nearby was a major train track that went south into Switzerland and west into France. This railway track was used for the transport of soldiers and supplies. Many bombs missed their target and fell on the residential neighborhoods instead.

Most houses on our street stood like open dollhouses with roofs and facades blown away exposing living rooms, bedrooms, torn and tattered flowery wallpaper, paintings hanging crooked on the walls, lace curtains blowing in the breeze, ghostly shadows of the people who had lived there.

At least for a while, innocence shielded children from the memories that came up for the adults in these ruins as they remembered the neighbors who had lived and died in those houses. For children, it was a forbidden playground, dangerous because of *Blindgänger,* dud bombs that had been dropped but had not exploded. Many were still found decades later during construction projects.

There were treasures to be found in the rubble of war, a risky adventure. One sunny day, I was digging, scratching with a stick of burned wood in the dirt piles of a burned-out building. I uncovered something metallic—a tiny little shoe, a leg, pants, a head with two big ears, a mouse face—Micky Mouse! I had found a treasure in the rubble—a bunch of small Micky Mouse pins held together with a wire!

I had met Mickey Mouse in comic books given to the children by American soldiers. Excited, I ran home with my treasure, to show my mother. But how had these pins arrived in the rubble of a ruined apartment building? Had they dropped from the sky with the bombs? My mother's fear made me throw the pins away; she thought Mickey Mouse might explode in my hands.

Many years later in graduate school, we were given the assignment to make a painting or drawing about a memory that haunted us. I made a drawing of fallen statues and ruined buildings with a superimposed Micky Mouse image. I had found a photograph of our street after the bombs and collaged it into the drawing along with a statue of the Kaiser on horseback. The next day in the seminar, during the show-and-tell time, I did not show or tell. I could not talk about that time. I am told that children often cannot talk about trauma but can draw pictures about it. I was not a child anymore then, but still, I could not talk about my surreal experience witnessing the destruction of life juxtaposed with "Micky Mouse."

Micky in the Ruins, pastel/collage

In 1948 and 1949, Germany was slowly waking up from the nightmare of war and the aftermath. The Nürnberg Nazi trials took place. Destroyed cities were being rebuilt. There was much grief over the loss of life—family members and friends—along with the trauma of a country lost in delusion and lies.

Quote "In the early years of the Federal Republic, Konrad Adenauer, as first Chancellor for the Republic, switched focus from denazification to recovery and led his country from the ruins of World War II to becoming a productive and prosperous nation that forged close relations with France, the United Kingdom, and the United States. During his years in power, West Germany achieved democracy, stability, international respect, and economic prosperity ("Wirtschaftswunder," German for "economic miracle"). Unquote" [Wikipedia]

We returned to the city. Our apartment building had been spared major damage from the bombings except for a fire in the roof; it was one of the few buildings on our street still standing. After a long time, schools opened again; America helped with school lunches. I remember the white mushy Wonder Bread and the smells of the soup kitchen.

Our teachers did not talk about the war in class; traumatized, they did not approach the subject. I heard discussions on the radio about the war and the Holocaust, but there were no answers for how all this could have happened, there was collective guilt, trauma, and denial. Adults were trying to understand what had been done and how the Holocaust could have happened in a country where philosophy and the arts are treasured. Guilt is a heavy burden, and many adults went into denial—"we did not know." The Treaty of Versailles at the end of World War One in 1919 was often mentioned, especially how unfair it had been to Germany. Often mentioned were aspect of Hitler's accomplishments—he built the Autobahn and created jobs after the depression. This was the excuse for racism, the killing of millions, and setting Europe on fire? Children were listening and watching.

I read *The Diary of Anne Frank* when I was ten years old. Her statement that she believed in the good in people despite what she and her family endured during their years of hiding. Her words, her Schicksal, her fate, had an enormous impact on me. I asked my mother about the Holocaust and what she knew about it. She told me this story: One night she woke up, there were loud noises, cars, and shouting outside. She went to see what was going on and saw our neighbors, the Jewish family that lived across the street coming out of the building with uniformed men. The parents and the three young, redheaded, beautiful girls were being taken from their apartment by the Gestapo. As they were pushed into the van, the father looked around for help. He saw my mother upstairs in the window and raised his fist in a helpless gesture. The family never returned. I asked Mother why she had not done anything. She said with a tearful voice, "What could I do? I had three small children myself. They would have taken us too."

16 | GROWING WINGS

JOURNAL ENTRY

NEW MEXICO

PRIVATE DESPAIR

I woke this morning carrying the burden of a dark night of dreams I don't remember. I tend to hold on to emotions. I struggle. I want to leave them behind. "Emotional discipline"—how easy to say but so difficult to do.

I listen to the Sunday-morning program on classical radio celebrating Memorial Day. I do not know this music, but I am strongly affected by the sweetness, grief, and strength of it. Weeping, I think about the Holocaust, a seemingly unrelated thought, a fleeting thought, yet deeply ingrained and very familiar to me on my life's journey. To my surprise, I learn from the announcement that this piece of music had been created for and played at a Holocaust memorial in 1996 somewhere I don't remember. How amazing for art to do this. I am really surprised it can be that specific. I think the source of my despair today may come from memories engrained in every fiber of my body. Abandonment and fear of not having enough have been my lifelong nemeses. Yet here and now I have so much!

I Am Falling,

monotype

CHAPTER 8

GOING TO THE RACES

My father was working in his garage again, now repairing the American officers' cars. He had made a friendly connection with Mr. C., an American officer stationed in Stuttgart. Mr. C., a professor of literature in America, often came to our apartment with a box of chocolate bars, chewing gum, or vanilla ice cream, all things we'd never had before. We ate up all the ice cream right away because we did not have a refrigerator. While we laughed and giggled with pleasure, enjoying that miraculous sweet melting treat, Mr. C. would sit down at our piano and play Chopin.

On Sundays, my father, the master mechanic, worked on a race car he had designed, building it with the help of his assistants and apprentices. One of his friends was a well-known race car driver, a German champion on the racetracks, which were opening again after the war.

Father had built the winning race car for his friend and probably thought, *If Karl Kling can win with the car I built for him, I can too—win that is!* So, after years of the trauma of war, he followed his bliss. He went about building his race car. His garage was a block away from our apartment. We were not allowed to go there during the workweek, but on Sundays, when the garage was closed for business, Papa used the space to build his dream, a race car, and we could visit.

Sunday Visit,

photo of the crew and the girls

One Sunday morning, Mutti went into the kitchen to bake pastries she called *Russen*, a yeast dough rolled up with cinnamon, hazelnuts, and sugar. She would cut the roll in half lengthwise, and two short strips of dough were laid across each other like a Russian Orthodox cross. The smell of freshly baked pastry was our Sunday "perfume." We happily took the snack to the garage where my father and his assistants worked. The smell of grease, black hands, happy faces, and the image of the skeleton of the engine and body of a developing car left a deeply engrained memory for me. Today, when I walk into Sam's Garage in Pecos, New Mexico, I remember those Sundays.

In 1948 and 1949, the first German automobile races were organized. Many of the race car drivers were not yet sponsored by the big car manufacturers like Mercedes or Porsche. Individual drivers built their race cars motivated by their passion in *Eigenbau* (self-made), supported by family and friends. "Our" race car was a beauty—a sleek design in shining silver. It had a number eight on its side when my father took it to the races. As I found out during my research for this book on the internet, Papa was a pioneer of the postwar racing scene with the car he built himself. He finished second and third in major races in Karlsruhe, Hockenheim, and the Schottenring, a racetrack near Schotten.

The racetrack closer to where we lived was "Solitude," a serious racetrack laid out in a large forest near Stuttgart, named after the nearby Schloss Solitude, a hunting castle built by one of the kings in a previous century.

We, as a family, could sit in the bleachers to watch the race! There was a strong spirit of comradery between the drivers. They were friends and shared their experiences with each other. It was a real buddy system. I remember many of the names mentioned at the dinner table, and drop-in visits to our apartment. My father's competitive spirit toward his champion friend Karl Kling was a strong motivation for him. During the race, the two kept challenging each other, showing off their driving skills. Wearing overalls, aviator goggles, and caps that covered their ears resembling fighter pilots. As they passed each other in their open race cars, they would look over to one another with grins and maybe even wave.

At the Start,

photo of father

BRIGITTE BRÜGGEMANN | 21

We watched the cars whizzing by from the stands near the finishing line. We saw my dad maintain first position for a while. But in the last round, he slipped to second, leaving first place to his friend who had saved some of his best tricks for last.

After the car races were finished, the motorcycles raced. The smell of burned rubber, the screeching sound of the bikes going around at high speed, the drivers leaning into the curve at a precarious angle, was too frightening for me. I could not watch it.

We were allowed to buy a bratwurst. I went with my sisters below the bleachers to eat my delicious wurst. I looked up to see Mutti sitting, forlorn, next to my father's secretary, whom we suspected had a relationship with my father other than a working relationship. I remember sadness, a feeling of abandonment and betrayal washing over me, I was mirroring and taking on what I thought was going on with Mutti, her feelings of betrayal.

#8 at the Races,

photo of father

The next big race for my father was at the Nürburg Ring, a famous German racecourse. Before he left with his crew, he gave my mother five Deutsche Mark; he and his coworkers had all chipped in to play the soccer lottery. They had figured out a system of odds for which team would win that next week. My dad had taken the last of our money to go to the race. Mutti decided not to play the lottery as she had been asked to do. Instead, she bought food for us. That weekend those teams she was to play were winning teams! I imagine my mother wondered how to tell father that she had not played.

The race was broadcast on the radio; we sat around the radio listening to the sportscaster. My dad was doing well; he was running in first place for quite a few rounds. Then, in an excited voice, the announcer reported that my father—car number eight—was not coming around! He had dropped out. We did not know what happened for a while. We were thinking the worst. Finally, the announcer said there had been an accident. My father had hit an oil slick in a curve on the track and had spun out of control. His car had flipped three times and landed upside down in a marshy meadow. It was announced that he was seriously injured and might not survive. We waited for news. He survived the crash but was badly hurt and was hospitalized for weeks. My mother did not have the means to travel many miles to see him.

I came home from school one day to find a stranger in our living room standing by the piano. He was very thin and wore a dark, elegant suit. I did not recognize my father. He was changed forever by that accident. He decided not to race anymore. The race car was sold. The new owner died in a fatal crash in his first race with car number eight. For many years, my father held on to a trophy he had won racing.

CHAPTER 9

ROLLER COASTER

My sister was given new roller skates, and with a snicker, she generously gave me her old skates. The skates had wooden wheels and did not roll very easily, but I was so happy to have them. I taught myself to skate in circles in front of our apartment building. We had a wide sidewalk with many patches of broken cement, but some places had not been destroyed by bombings and still provided smooth surfaces.

With my roller skates strapped to my shoes, I made my circles, putting one foot across in front of the other to make curves. After a little practice, that went pretty well. Then I dared myself to play airplane, lifting one foot out behind me and stretching both arms out like wings as I went round and round, free of all childhood troubles.

Across the street was a terraced garden owned and cultivated by the local greengrocer. As I was skating, a gardener looked up from her plantings and watched me with a smile on her face. Then water came down on me! Frau Lange, who lived on the ground floor of our building, was upset about the noise the skates made. She threw water from her window to douse me, but inadvertently, she threw the pitcher out with the water! It crashed onto the pavement. I kept making my circles.

The last few years of my parents' marriage was very difficult for them and for us children as well. My father was abusive, angered easily, and was violent towards my mother and my older sisters. I do not remember that he spent time playing with us or encouraging us to learn, but he demanded that we must be quiet when he listened to the radio program that reported the Sunday soccer game. It was no secret that he had a mistress. He left us often, even on Christmas Eve, the most treasured family time in the year. He was unavailable—a no show—for us children and my mother.

Mutti was despondent; she cried a lot. I tried to console her by holding on to her apron as she was standing by the stove cooking. She often suffered from terrible headaches and stayed in bed for days. I would bring her a cold washcloth to put on her forehead and sit on the edge of her bed wanting her to feel better.

One night, she left the house. I was in my bed, pretending I was in a boat in rough waters but safe. I worried that she might be going up to the train track near our house. The fast train to Zürich would go by at nine thirty in the evening. I knew she was thinking of ending her pain. She came back that night and gently hugged us.

Another evening some weeks later, she lovingly put us to bed and quietly closed the door. Later I learned from my older sister that she had stuffed newspaper in the cracks between the door and the frame and then put tape around the doorframe. Late in the night, my sisters and I heard our father come home. There was screaming and shouting. My mother had opened the gas in the kitchen range; she was crouched with her head in the oven breathing in the deadly gas when he found her. He pulled her out, still conscious, and in his fury, he beat her badly.

In the morning, for the first and only time ever, he took us to school in his car. I went into my classroom, put my head on my desk, and cried. My second-grade teacher asked my mother to come in for a conference.

1948,

Brigitte, 6 years old

CHAPTER 10

CHRISTMAS

A particular Christmas for a child can be a milestone, the highlight of the year. I do not remember many Christmases, but memories of several stayed with me—the good ones infused with the "spirit of Christmas" as they say, when redemption is possible, families gather, and love is tangible.

This was the most magical one I remember: In Germany, the freshly cut Christmas tree is set up on Christmas Eve and stays up for twelve days until January 6, the day the three kings guided by a star, found the child in the manger, as goes the story. That Christmas eve my father and a friend of his, in a rare display of family togetherness, bundled us in the car and drove into the woods. It was a snowy day with a few inches on the ground. The winter forest was beautiful. Tall evergreens were covered with snow, and the cold air was crackling. We drove down a narrow, snowy forest road to find our tree.

The perfect tree was found, the men cut it down and put into the car. Just as we piled back into the vehicle, squeezing in with the tree, the forest guardian pulled up behind us. I do not remember how my father solved the situation, but we were allowed to take the tree home.

Later that day, as it was getting dark outside, we children were led into the kitchen, which was filled with the aroma of Lebkuchen still baking in the oven. The kitchen door closed behind us, Mother and Father disappeared. Soon we heard a little bell ringing. The door to the living room opened, the magical moment was here! We saw the tree decorated with lit candles, the warm glow of the flames illuminating the room. And there, waiting under the tree, were gifts for each of us.

In the magical candlelight, I saw a playhouse grocery store. There was a little counter that held a tiny cash register with toy money. Next to it was a miniature scale and little baskets containing marzipan fruit and vegetables—potatoes, miniature carrots, and cauliflower. There was a shelf behind the counter that provided a space where, I imagined, I could stand as the salesperson, while my sisters played the roles of customers. The shelf was filled with containers and small drawers that held miniature candies, macarons, and other precious little food items.

Christmas Eve,

etching

Before we could touch anything, we sang Christmas songs and listened to my mother reading the nativity story from the Bible. My father was a shadow in the background; he was not participating. I wondered what he was thinking then.

My mother asked for a divorce a few years after that holiday. She had suffered greatly in a marriage that was not based on equality and loving mutual support. The marriage had become violent and abusive.

On a cold winter day, I stood by the frosted-over kitchen window. I drew pictures with my finger in the frosty ice blooms on the glass, circles and arrows taking me into another reality. I heard Mother at the front door telling our neighbor, an elderly, friendly woman, that the divorce had been granted. I was sad and relieved at the same time; I had been afraid of my father. I would hide behind a stuffed chair when he came home.

Years later, after my father was gone, Mutti was always reluctant to celebrate Christmas. She did not want a tree; the preparations seem to bring painful memories for her. One year, on Christmas Eve morning, it looked like, once again "it" was not going to happen. We did not have a tree. I had saved up one Deutsche Mark in my piggy bank. With the silver coin clutched in my hand, I ran to the Christmas tree market that had been set up near my school. The merchant was getting ready to close shop and had already put all trees that had not sold onto a pile to be loaded. With a smile and a "frohe Weihnachten," the man gave me the tree for my one Deutsche Mark.

I was proud to bring the tree home. Creating a different outcome to a situation made me happy. I felt so grown up! My sisters and I set the tree up in the corner of the living room. We put candles and decorations on it, laughed, and admired the beautiful ornaments. The climax was the little porcelain angel destined to go to the top of the tree to bless us all.

At five in the evening, we put some candles in the window and went to church for the candlelight service for children and families. Our church had been bombed and burned out but had been rebuilt in the fifties. It was built in a very simple, clean, white brick architectural style that was common for Lutheran churches. We sat in the pew watching the caretaker light the candles on the huge Christmas tree that almost reached the ceiling of the church. Candle after candle was lit with another candle attached to the end of a long stick.

The church was packed. Everyone was quietly watching. It was now dark outside. Candles attached to the end of each pew created a beautiful glow in the church. It was a truly silent night, a holy night. The youth choir—with my two sisters included—was performing. Bach, organ music was followed by a nativity play that told the story of Christmas. I had a part in the play. Dressed in my new pink flannel nightgown, I played the angel announcing to the shepherds that Christ was born. My announcement was in the form of a song "*From Himmel hoch da komm ich her.*" I was nervous but so excited to sing that song in front of the whole congregation. On a high note, my voice broke, and I saw my sister up in the choir snicker.

When the service was over, outside in the cold night air, trumpets played "*Oh, du fröhliche oh du selige Weihnachtszeit.*" My mother, my sisters, and I walked home holding on to each other. All was good. Peace was there with us. The candles in our windows beckoned. We had oranges and tangerines, potato salad, and Vienna sausages for our traditional Christmas Eve dinner.

CHAPTER 11

HARD TIMES—FIRST CALLING

When I was in elementary school in third and fourth grade, my favorite subject was art. I loved to draw, it made me happy. When I got my grades, I was very disappointed that I had a "*2–Gut*" (a B) in art, the only subject I cared about. I cried. Herr Siebert, the teacher, called me to his desk and asked with a kind voice, "What is the matter?" I do not remember if I was able to give him an answer because of my tears, but he changed the grade to a "*Sehr Gut*"—an A—with a knowing smile, just like that!

With the divorce "trouble" had gone out the door, we were happy to have peace; but it was a hard time financially. Father hardly supported us, he disappeared, moved away without a word for a time. He had his own business and several employees; his clients had loved him. Maybe he could not deal with the loss of his dream to be a race car champion. He became unreliable in business; his longtime clients stayed away. Finally, he gave up, closed his business, and without a word to say good-bye, found a job in Bavaria.

Mutti managed in miraculous ways, sometimes selling her jewelry and other valuable things from her dowry. She had very little support from our extended family. When her parents' ruined house was sold—it had been bombed and burned down in the last days of the war—she had a little inheritance to keep us going. Divorce at the time held a stigma for women, and mother often felt ostracized.

We still had access to my grandparents' magical garden on the edge of Mutti's hometown. It was filled with fruit trees and berry bushes. We had to take a train ride and then walked several miles from the station up the hill. At the end of the day, we would return home with baskets filled with fruits and berries for making jam and conserves.

A beautiful iron gate decorated with my grandfather's initials gave entrance to paradise by using a large iron key to open the heavy gate. There was a mysterious round gazebo in the center of the garden with a musky smell inside. My grandfather, a respected professional painter and guild master, had painted centaurs all around the inside walls. He must have loved Greek mythology, as I do.

Grandfather died in his fifties, still in the prime of his life. He did not have to experience another war though; he had fought and was injured in WWI in France. He was buried in the garden next to the gazebo. I felt his presence in the garden even though I never knew him. My grandmother carried on through the rise of Hitler, strong soul that she was she lived in the patched up ruined house for a few more years after the war. She passed away when I was just a toddler. I remember her tall, elegant figure, her bright-red velvet sofa standing in the only livable place in the ruin, and the beautiful roses she grew, which my grandfather had painted.

In the garden, my sisters and I loved to climb the apple tree, each of us claiming a specific branch that "had our name on it." I loved to lie in the wildflower meadows that were filled with daisies and blue campanulas. The berry bushes—red, white and black currents—and the tall pear tree all left me with a love and a craving for the taste of those fruits and berries. My love for nature and its mystery started there in that garden. That garden became a "Paradise Lost" for me until I found it again in New Mexico and in my paintings.

Brigitte In Grandmother's Garden,

photo collage

JOURNAL ENTRY

NEW MEXICO

Some days my soul is floating on the surface of my consciousness like a fish coming up for air. Today is such a day. A simple phrase—forget me not—called up some childhood memories and images of my grandmother's garden: her flowery meadow, an abundance of flowers so deep I could lie down in them and disappear into another reality. Forget-me-nots, lily of the valley, daisies, violets, and was there not something pink, and yes, the yellow rose? The language of flowers, mysterious and metaphorical, calling out the names of women and lives lived, not in this world but from it. I must awake today to find what the fish was coming up to find. What is it I must remember?

Orchard,

watercolor

To help our finances, Mutti had managed to get a contract with a magazine publisher to distribute magazine subscriptions door to door and collect the payments. Piles of magazines were stacked up on our dining room table. Mutti and the three of us children each had routes for delivering the magazines. Up the stairs down the stairs and, once a month, collect the subscription money. Ring the doorbells and wait. I was around ten or eleven years old then and proud to be of help.

My uncle had emigrated to America during the depression. Occasionally, we received a care package from him, a miracle—spam, chocolate, other nonperishables, and clothes my aunt and cousin in Philadelphia did not use anymore. Those clothes seemed so glamorous to me, their colorful patterns, large swinging skirts conjuring up images and lifestyles of another world. Mutti transformed the adult-size dresses to make clothes for us.

One day when I was to collect payments, I happily wore my new sundress Mutti had made for me from one of those dresses with a pretty red and white flower pattern. I was especially excited because this dress was not the usual "hand-me-down" dress my sisters had outgrown. This was just for me! I found a little necklace to go with the dress, and all dressed up, I went to collect the monthly bill from a family living up on the sixth floor of an apartment building. I rang the doorbell, waited, and rang again. The door opened, and a woman looked me up and down with disdain. "What do you want from me if you can dress like that?" And she slammed the door on me. I slowly walked down those stairs holding back tears.

34 | GROWING WINGS

CHAPTER 12

LOST IN THE FOREST

My mother loved hunting for mushrooms and made delicious meals for us with those wonderful-smelling beauties. Often, we went into the forest with a group led by a guide, a kind man who knew his mushrooms. We would meet at a point in a forest at the edge of town and then spread out for the hunt with our little baskets.

My memory of this day is still very vivid: a dark fairytale forest—the Hänsel and Gretel kind— and mysterious events unfolding. My mother was helping an elderly person up the slope. I was following my sister's hiking boots, a few feet ahead of me, going up a slope covered with pine needles and slippery moist leaves, my eyes focused on the ground looking for mushrooms. Suddenly I found myself alone with nobody in sight. I kept walking faster, trying to find the group, but I soon realized I was lost in the forest, and I was frightened.

Then, just like in a puppet show, a man popped out of a ditch. He looked like an elf out of a storybook, short with a rounded belly. "Why are you crying?" he asked. I told him I was looking for the mushroom hunters. He said that he was looking for that group also, and we would both look for them together. I was so relieved to have found a helper.

Soon we came upon a snack bar by a soccer field, a resting place for people hiking in the forest. The people showed concern for me, I was crying again. They asked me to stay with them until the mushroom hunters showed up there. I was afraid of their big German shepherd, and I said I wanted to walk on with the man.

We heard in a distance the calling of my name, but the man told me to be quiet. He did not call back. He said that he knew where they were, and we would join up with the group soon. We went on taking the path to the city leading us out of the forest. I felt something was not right and became more and more quiet.

After a long walk, we came into the city. I recognized the neighborhood not far from where we lived. I took off running, ran all the way home to our house about thirty blocks away. When I got home, my sister opened the door. She was standing in the front hall looking in the mirror combing her hair. She told me, distracted by her own image in the mirror, that Mother had called the police to look for me with search dogs.

I was still standing by the front door feeling I had done something wrong, when my mother came back, accompanied by the police, to fetch a piece of clothing for the search dogs to take in my scent. Mutti was so relieved to find me at home! She asked me a hundred questions as she shed tears and held me tight. The police insisted that she examine me to see if I had been abused.

A week earlier, a little girl my age had disappeared from her neighborhood and was never found. Many years later, the remains of a little girl were found in a basement in the very neighborhood I had recognized when I ran away. A man, after decades, was arrested and confessed to have killed this little girl. This story is still a mystery to me. Was that man an elf or a murderer? Choosing to run, to escape, to find my way home may have saved my life to live.

"Home" became a metaphor for the path to safety and the self for me. This experience in my young life activated my ability to make self-empowering decisions I would call on often when I needed to take special care of myself and, at times, make life-changing choices.

PART 2
FINDING MY PATH

CHAPTER 13

SOUL SEARCHING

At the age of sixteen, I started to think about what I wanted "to do" in my life. What could my profession, my livelihood, be? My mother was supportive but passive in her guidance, letting me find my way. I knew I would have only myself to fall back on to sustain me in the future.

The city offered a counseling service to help young people figure out possibilities for the future and help to find out what they were good at to determine their educational path. I had always liked my art classes best in school and had a deep yearning to be creative in some way. I was told in very blunt ways by that counselor, that to be an artist, one must be a genius and would probably starve in the process. To this day, I feel the despair I felt then. The person behind that big, dark-brown, wooden desk gave me no encouragement or helpful suggestions at all.

I kept searching for a meaningful pathway to earn a living. I wanted to do something creative, to do something I love to do.

JOURNAL ENTRY

NEW MEXICO

I ask the same question I asked myself back then as a young girl: What is at my core right now? Another way to ask: What is the color of my soul? Today, more than ever my soul seeks the light. I am very aware of that surge to consciousness, to seek my truth and what this life is about for me.

Making, creating—that is my joy and greatest pleasure. It may not always be about painting an image. It is about shaping my thoughts, my environment and who I am. Spending much time alone helps in that process, with awareness watching urges and desires come up, bringing thought into words, images, form, and action. There is the "doing" of the body and the restlessness of the mind, but most important is the "being," is it not? With creative doing, joy is coming into my being. Creating brings energy into my day coming from another place. It is not about creating a masterpiece. Of course, I am thrilled when I get a "good one," but creating is more about getting in touch with this other reality that I cannot speak about. I can only catch a glimpse of it: stardust, a ray of light falling through some trees. And suddenly I see a million small particles dancing in it.

I loved to sew my clothes. I had watched my mother often. At night, I would wake up and hear the buzz of her sewing machine. I would sneak out of bed and sit across from her, watching her every move until she sent me back to bed.

As a young woman, I asked myself, *why not fashion design?* That sounded exciting and "practical." I knew I could not go to university, or the Academy of Arts. The lack of money was a problem. At that time, higher education was not free. Also, in high school, I had a difficult time in my language classes— English and French. I could never remember the conjugations or the vocabulary; I could not relate to the abstract meaning. It was depressing to just barely pass each year. To go on for three more years to get a baccalaureate was not an option I considered. I wanted to go the alternative route to education available, which was a vocational training. It is ironic that I became fluent in English and French later when I was learning a language through day-to-day living, and a hands-on approach that has always been the best way for me to learn.

I explored the idea of learning the craft of seamstress and designer, including all elements of the process—designing, pattern making, learning about fabrics, and the actual putting together of the parts of a garment. A three-year apprenticeship in tailoring did not feel right to me because it would focus on the tedious, slavish making of garments and would not offer the creative design aspect. I wanted to learn more than the craft of needlework. I found out about a three-year school that sounded perfect because it offered all aspects of the craft and design. The problem was that I was not sixteen yet, the age requirement to enter the program.

For my mother, education was one of the most important things she felt she could give us; she always encouraged us to do the best we could do in our homework. She was in full support of my idea and went on her "warpath." She made an appointment to speak with the principal of the school, pleading with her to take me on. The principal, an elegant, tall, white-haired woman dressed in black, reminded me of my grandmother. To our great joy, she said yes! She wanted to give me a chance.

But there was another problem: I was still not even 16 years old, my father, from a distance, had to approve and continue to pay child support until I was eighteen. He himself had only a nine-year elementary school education. He was born and grew up in Alsace Lorraine, which was part of Germany at the time and during World War One. The Treaty of Versailles in 1919 made it once again part of France. My grandfather had been a policeman who—I think—had made some enemies during the war, a taboo subject that was never spoken off. My grandparents had to flee across the border into Germany, and my father's education was cut short. Young teenage Papa loved automobiles and became a car mechanic, doing the work he loved instead of a more extensive formal education.

My father objected to my plans to attend design school because he did not want to pay child support for two more years while I was in school. He suggested that, instead, I should work in a grocery store selling eggs and cheese! My oldest sister had finished her education with a baccalaureate at the time and had a good job. Feeling responsible for her little sister, she wrote a letter to Father pleading with him to allow me to undertake a creative vocational training. (I did not know this until I found that letter many years later in my mother's things after her passing). Father agreed grudgingly.

The next three years opened a door to my creative energy. Not only did I enjoy making and designing clothes, but I also made friends with my classmates, who were creative, free-spirited girls. I was still a child in so many ways. The other girls had boyfriends and were so much more "grown-up" than I was, but my joyful innocence drew them to me.

Part of the program was art history and design. The professor was lecturing on Greek art, which fascinated me. I was hooked on art! The design class was also a favorite class for me. We worked on color combinations, created color compositions, pushing fabric squares around until the composition of colors was just right. I saw and understood for the first time the relativity of color, how one color will influence the color placed next to it.

My spirits went high; I had a ball. I so enjoyed the creative part of designing. The craft part—the stitching and sewing part—I would have rather skipped through fast. My teacher would often say, "Nicht so schlampig, Fräulein" (Don't be so sloppy, Fräulein). I would laugh and keep skipping. It was the outcome that interested me.

After graduation, I wanted to go on toward fashion design, designing clothes and creating fashion collections in styles that changed with the seasons. The plan began with an internship with a clothing manufacturing plant for one year, then continued at another school where we would learn about the executive level of design and management. How I was to accomplish that part was not at all clear to me, but I decided to go just one step at the time.

The internship in a factory was probably the most difficult period in my young working life. As an intern, I was to float around to help keeping the flow on the assembly line. The workers, all women, had to do the same task over and over, all day long. They would complete the same steps on a garment, then pass it on to the next worker on the assembly line. I felt sorry for the women who had to do this boring, tedious work.

One of the women had gone to elementary school with me. She had not done well academically and had been an outsider in class. The workers, and this young woman especially, were resentful of my position and sabotaged my work in any way they could. The only two men on the floor, who created the patterns and cut the fabrics, ridiculed and discouraged my ambition. They made me believe the potential for a woman to rise to an executive position in the business was small, and maybe they were right. At the time most fashion designers were men. It was before the feminist movement; a woman in the early sixties had a way to go toward recognition in the business world.

I did not question the system. I just wanted to do something I loved to do—create something that had not been done before. At nineteen, I experienced my first existential crisis. I was confused and lost. I was so young, and not yet strong enough to stand up for myself in the cutthroat environment of the fashion industry. I quit the internship and was faced with the question: What now? I'd had had a purpose and direction for a while, but now it was clear I had to rethink my future.

JOURNAL ENTRY

NEW MEXICO

Smoke signals. It is a clear day, and I can see, can I? My life seems like a labyrinth that keeps me going round and round and sometimes takes unexpected turns. I come out the same place I was at years ago, but on closer inspection, I probably have moved over and up just a notch on the spiral of life.

My thoughts have been going and going, and I just can't figure things out, so I go out into the garden and do some work that will help me to stay focused on something real. Loneliness pushes in on me if I let it. I look up into the blue sky. Then I make a fire to warm my heart and spirit, to keep the bugs and worries away and send smoke signals to whom it may concern.

CHAPTER 14

PLAN B — 1962 STUTTGART

One day, as I aimlessly wandered around in town, I met my friend Barbara from the vocational design school from which we both had recently graduated. She told me that she too had decided not to pursue fashion design and had started an apprenticeship in an art gallery.

She talked about her experience in the gallery in glowing terms. I was intrigued by the idea since I had already discovered my love for art, so I decided to find out more about this possibility. I went to visit the gallery. I talked to Dr. Z., the owner, a kind man with a white beard and long hair, wearing Birkenstock sandals, unusual for a businessman at the time. He emanated such gentle energy that I wanted to be part of that family of people who worked there. I was hired as a three-year apprentice in the art department of the Kunsthaus.

There were different departments on each floor of the five-story building. On the first floor, materials to do with paper and writing were sold. On the second floor, fine arts and craft items were sold, lovely special jewelry, glass items, and beautiful handmade craft objects. This was Kunst-Handwerk, applied arts at its best. On the third floor, where I worked, prints of the masters, original graphic art, art books, minerals, and crystals were sold.

On the fourth floor, the work of regional painters and sculptors, masters of the region, were exhibited. I was fascinated by this space. It felt so special, almost sacred to me. I would sneak up there as often as I could. I loved to look at the paintings and absorb the subtle colors and textures of the impressionistic, expressive paintings of the regional southwest German landscape, the landscape I knew well and loved.

The painters would come to visit sometimes to talk to the staff members and bring in new work. They were part of the "family," and I was in awe of them. They were heroes to me. Most of them were men who painted recognizable imagery in an expressionistic style. Their work was not avant-garde but was very beautiful. We had vernissages—openings—that celebrated their new work. I was part of a world that recognized and honored the importance of art and beauty in our lives and culture.

BRIGITTE BRÜGGEMANN | 43

My fellow apprentices were my age. We became close and supportive of each other, we worked and partied together, looked at and learned about art, together. I learned so much by osmosis, by just looking.

Customers would come in to buy prints of famous paintings by the masters like Rembrandt, Monet, Van Gogh, Gauguin, Cézanne, Matisse, Picasso, Klee, and many others—"for over the sofa in the living room." I would show them the collections we had in those great big wooden file cabinets, helping clients find a painting they loved. At the end of the day, the apprentices had to sort all the prints back into the files. We played a game of guessing who the artist of the work was when it was still partially hidden behind the print on top. We could, at times, see only a strip of an inch or two of the work to guess at. We learned and taught each other to recognize the styles of different artists by just looking at small parts of the paintings.

The adults in the gallery were interesting people who ranged from manager types to passionate lovers of art. Apprentices were taught, chaperoned, and guided by them in a very loving way.

It was a magical time that showed me what was meaningful to me: friendship, love, and art. I acquired a sense for and recognition of style, quality, and depth of meaning. I continued to seek out art anywhere I could. I would learn about it and keep it in my heart. Art had become nourishment for my soul.

After my apprenticeship was over, one of my dreams came true: I traveled to Greece with a student group to see my first love up close: Greek art. I had a magical time in Athens, saw the Acropolis, the famous sculptures in the museums, Delphi, Olympia and Mycenae, the island of Crete with the Minoan temple in Knossos. I experienced the timelessness of art and the power of its presence over centuries.

CHAPTER 15

LEAVING THE NEST—PARIS 1964

After my journey to Greece—a journey of first independence—I decided to move to Paris to see more art and experience a different life and cultural environment. I wanted to leave behind the burdens of my childhood, my memories of growing up in a broken family, and the troubled history of the German people. I was running away to the new and unfamiliar, challenging my ability to find my way in a strange place and "survive."

I was the youngest of three girls. My closest connection was with my oldest sister, who was five years my senior. My relationship with my other sister, who was three years my senior, had been troubled by her fierce competitive spirit, not unusual for the middle child. She had always been closest to my father and had a very difficult time accepting the divorce.

My oldest sister had married a French man and permanently moved to Paris. She had truly been my "big sister," looking after me in various ways. We listened to classical music on her record player in a corner of our apartment. We had the sort of conversations a young teenager must have with an older one. She was, and still is today, supportive in her quiet, loving way. Because I missed her, and because I had such a desire and hunger for new experiences, I decided to move to Paris to be near her. I wanted to fly the coop but have her close by to watch me grow my wings.

Throughout my life, living in foreign countries, I have always felt a release from the cultural traditions I grew up with. I have experienced liberation from thoughts about what is possible and what is expected. I have felt the freedom to think outside the box.

As a foreigner, I feel like an outsider for a long, long time as I look into the window of a culture from the "outside," giving me the freedom to make decisions that might seem daring inside the cultural framework of my home country. I discovered that being different and on the "outside" is not necessarily a negative. Over time, over decades, I learned to accept and even enjoy my status as an "alien."

In 1964, in Paris at the age of twenty-two, I felt liberated from the past, but at the same time, I was very conscious about the history and the still-open wounds engendered by the war when Germany and France had been enemies. I was aware of and cautious around the understandable resentment toward Germans only twenty years after that war. Memories were still fresh of what had been done by the Nazis to the people of France.

The challenges were at times difficult. I had to make important and necessary adjustments for assimilation—learning a language, understanding different customs and behavior patterns, accepting differences, overcoming ethnocentricity, and enduring awkward moments of being a stranger in a foreign country. My horizon was expanding, and my social skills were adapting and improving.

I was curious about France, and Paris in particular. Germany and France in the fifties and sixties, had built a friendship after a history of war and animosity between the two cultures. Germany's first chancellor after the war, Konrad Adenauer, had started a conversation with Charles De Gaulle, president of France. Cultural exchanges had become popular. Germans loved French food and a more joyful way of life, sitting in outdoor cafes and bistros with friends, enjoying a glass of wine or an espresso.

Travel for Germans in the late fifties and sixties had almost become an obsession. Germans had money to go places. The *Wirtschaftswunder* (the economic miracle) had made a huge change in people's financial situations, and curiosity made other countries like Italy, Spain, and France, very popular. Germans were seeking sunny climates and cultures that were different from what they knew. The war had changed Germans' outlook on life; they wanted to leave behind the dark memories and start over with a more open lifestyle. The French also had to come to terms with their history of collaboration by the Vichy government with the Nazis, antisemitism, and persecution of French Jews.

That very dark period in German history changed the culture dramatically: progressive thinking became a path to overcome that past, to not forget that history, to never let Fascism happen again, to be supportive and tolerant of minorities, to support free higher education, and to develop a social network that helps people in need. This may not be in the consciousness of the younger generations as much as it certainly is for my generation who lived through the war and postwar eras.

CHAPTER 16

FINDING A LANDING PLACE

I found an au pair position with a young French family who lived near the Boulevard du Montparnasse. The wife was a native of Berlin, Germany. I was to look after the little boy, and I shared a room with the child in the small apartment. Even though, when I was growing up, I did not have my own room, now at age twenty-two, I found it difficult to share my personal space with a little boy and be in charge of most of the household. I longed for more freedom.

After a short stay with the family, I looked for a different option. I found an advertisement in the paper offering a room in exchange for some housework and German lessons for the teenage daughter of the family. They lived on the Quai Anatole-France next to what later became the Musée D'Orsay, a fabulous, elegant neighborhood across from the Tuileries and the Louvre, overlooking the Seine, a short walk to the Place de la Concorde. How lucky could I get!

My room was on the sixth floor, which had formerly been the servants' floor. Entering the house through the back servants' door, I climbed up a winding staircase to a small room just large enough to hold a single bed and a small table. A French door opened over the rooftops of Paris with the Eiffel Tower like a mysterious guardian in the distance!

The apartments on the first five floors in the building were accessed through a separate, much more elegant entrance and an elevator. The shaft for the elevator cables went through my room along the ceiling. I heard the churning of the elevator cables above my head. Doves nested in the shaft, and their cooing noises were reassuring and poetic to me. I found my situation rather charming and romantic. The shared bathroom on my floor was out in the hallway. It was a traditional old-fashioned French toilet—a hole in the floor! The toilet also served as a shower: when the chain to flush was pulled, water would come from the top down, and one had to either take a shower or run. I preferred however, once a week, to go to the local bathhouse for a generous bath. I'd visit the local farmers' markets twice a week, mostly for the smells and sights. I enjoyed the vendors in their colorful stalls, their laughter and shouting, the people selecting their fruit and vegetables while in animated conversation with the vendors. Myself, for lack of funds, I made mostly due with the wonderful baguettes from the boulangerie at the corner.

I worked for two hours every morning cleaning the office space of the lady of the house, a psychiatrist. I had to clean the waiting room and her office, which overlooked the Seine. She had furnished her office with lovely antique furniture, and I fondly remember a Picasso drawing in a frame on her Louis XIV desk.

On the first floor of the building lived Pierre Cardin, the famous fashion designer whose work and style I had admired for years. I would pass below his windows when crossing the courtyard for the back staircase and the servants' entry. I would sometimes see Monsieur Cardin standing by the window looking out, a romantic figure to me. I contemplated asking him for a job. I never did. I knew unconsciously that my path was leading me somewhere else.

This arrangement turned out to be a very good situation because I could go to school every morning at the Alliance Française, studying French. I just had to find a little job for money for a few groceries. In class, Americans, Italians, Spanish, English, Germans were all learning together. We could speak only French; we had to learn fast. I met a fellow student working for the German Embassy. He invited me to go to the Club Alliance Française where many students met, partied, danced to the music, and became friends in a foreign country.

The young German (I secretly called him The Ambassador) helped me find a job with Lufthansa, the German Airline, in the city office near the Place de la Concorde. It was a part-time job sorting papers, organizing the mail, and doing other small tasks. It was enough to buy my baguette and cover my basic needs every day. I got by with little else.

My sister lived outside of Paris. I visited her whenever I could, or we would meet in town for coffee or a snack after she got off work. We went to concerts and museums together, and we talked about books she was reading about French history and politics. To help me out with a little money, she commissioned me to sew some clothes for her, which I enjoyed doing.

It was exciting to live in Paris. There was so much art to see and so many things to do! Soon a friend from Stuttgart joined me in Paris. She too was an au pair girl, and we spent time together sharing our trials and tribulations. Not having any money did not at all worry me. I lived one day at a time.

One night at the club of the Alliance Française, I met another young German man. We started to date and fell in love, spending much time together, exploring the beautiful city so perfect for romance. I had not had any lasting romantic relationship before, so being in love was new to me. At times it was overwhelming to try to figure out what our path would be together. His focus was very much on his career in the hotel business. He worked at the finest five-star hotel in Paris at the Place Vendome.

Art was not on his list of interests; he loved the Beatles and rock and roll music. We shared and learned from each other. After just a few months, he moved to Switzerland for the winter season, and then on to London to another five-star hotel. I received a letter from him almost every day, which kept the romance alive from a distance.

I found another part-time job as a tourist guide in Paris for German tourists and was working more hours at Lufthansa, all of which made my finances a bit more secure. I was challenged to find ways to make things work. I managed to live frugally and soon moved into a little apartment I loved. It was furnished with just a few necessary pieces and had a beautiful large French door framing the vista of the Eiffel Tower, now even closer than before. My life was filled with friends and new experiences.

I visited the museums often: The Louvre, the Orangerie, and the Jeu de Pomme, showing the Impressionist and the twentieth-century collection. To this day, I love Monet's *Waterlilies* in the Orangerie. I go to see them every time I have a chance to visit Paris. Maybe today I see the paintings with more understanding and recognition of the painter's craft and genius than I did back then, but the experience was thrilling then as it is now.

Monet was commissioned to paint those amazing, magical abstract paintings for two large oval rooms. The paintings are attached to the walls like a mural following the curves of the walls. The viewer is inside that circle—"inside" the pond. I love the drawing of lines into the transparent fields of color creating movement and depth. Each painting has a slightly different color palette, from dark blues and greens to luminous blues, greys, and yellows. Even though the paintings are quite abstract, there is much to suggest trees, flowers, water, and light to hold our recognition as well as inviting our imagination. Looking at original paintings by famous masters I had only seen as prints before made my life so rich. I always felt uplifted and had a spring in my step after looking at those paintings and sculptures.

Degas, today, an encounter at the Musée D'Orsay

I did not know at that time just how much influence and inspiration I would carry with me from those experiences—the colors, the textures, and the motives. Connecting emotionally and passionately with what I saw stayed with me and helped me to find my voice to speak about beauty without apology

JOURNAL ENTRY

NEW MEXICO

The precious process of painting:

I believe that color in a painting, even without an image, creates vibrations in the soul that leads to emotions and associations. I think for me, emotion comes before conscious thought. Color can make me feel any range of emotions. I am drawn to harmony. This is true for music, poetry, and paintings. Disharmony—arrangement of forms and color in a jarring way—can work in art if there is "resolution" worked into the composition. I want resolution; I want harmony, in form, composition, and color.

CHAPTER 17

WALKABOUT

I enjoyed life in Paris. On my way to work in the mornings, I would stop at the bistro to get *un café et un croissant* fresh from the *boulangerie*. I visited the bouquinistes along the Seine, selling antiquarian books and etchings, treasures to be found. It was fun to be around the many young people in the French Quarter, living in the *Quartier Latin*, strolling the Boulevard St. Michel until late at night, the jazz clubs, the *chansonniers* in the smoke-filled basements packed with people listening to the *chansons* about life, love, and sorrow. Sometimes I stayed up with friends till the early morning hours. We'd go to Les Halles—the "stomach of Paris"—a wholesale grocery market in a beautiful huge glass domed building in the center of Paris. (Unfortunately, it has been taken down and moved to make room for a nondescript shopping mall.) There was hustle and bustle there—vendors shouting, the sounds of buying and selling of vegetables, fruits, whole sides of meat, fish, poultry, cheese—anything to go to grocery stores, restaurants, and hotels all over Paris.

It was such fun to walk the aisles and listen to the sounds, smell the smells, and, yes, there were flower stalls too—my favorites. To crown the experience, the custom was to have a bowl of French onion soup with croutons and melted cheese on top. Then we'd find our way home after a night on the town and get some sleep. I have seen many cities and places since, but when I visit Paris today, I realize it is still my favorite city in the world. I ask myself a question that is difficult to answer: Why did I ever leave? Maybe because the river goes to the ocean?

After two years in Paris, I was still connected to my boyfriend from Germany in a distant sort of way. When he announced his move to London, I decided to go with him without thinking much about the consequences of having to establish myself again in another foreign country. My school English was not very good. I had to learn another language, English, a language that could be useful in the future.

In London, another au pair position was my landing point. Very quickly it became clear to me that I was being taken advantage of—I was working as a "girl Friday." In exchange for room and board and some pocket money, I had the duties of a maid. Most importantly, I was not given time for school to study the language. I fled. I left that family.

52 | GROWING WINGS

There was a time of uncertainty, but I had reached out earlier to the German airline Lufthansa, in London. A generous recommendation from the Lufthansa office in Paris smoothed my way to a position in London. How grateful I was to have landed on my feet again!

Having a real job, I had to find a place to live—a room of my own, a challenge in a big busy city like London. I had to be creative. My way to find accommodations was ringing the intercom button on each apartment building where I thought there might be a room available. Speaking into the intercom, I'd say, "Do you have room to let?" To my big surprise, my question was answered one day by an Irish lady, Mrs. Kane, with "Come on up!" A nice bright room was offered to me as a result of knocking on doors.

I worked hard to learn the language, reading the newspaper headlines, watching shows on my rented TV, and keeping my eyes and ears open. I was in swinging '60s London, a time in England dominated by "flower power," the Rolling Stones, the Beatles, and other groups that were also famous all over the world. A weekly program on TV with David Frost, TV host and journalist, informed me about what was new and exciting in the United Kingdom.

I was working in telephone reservations, making friends with colleagues, working side by side as part of a team in a large room answering the phones. In the '60s, airline reservations were done without computers. All information on flights came from big, fat schedule books and large blackboards showing the constantly changing status of flights. I learned by listening and watching others. My English was improving, but it was not that great yet. Whenever a client called and spoke to me with a heavy American accent, I had trouble understanding. I would, if possible, pass the phone to Erika who was working next to me and had taken me under her wings.

One exciting benefit to working for an airline was that I could travel at a fraction of the cost of a regularly priced ticket. I saw exotic places like India, Thailand, Africa, Italy, and Turkey. I would go for weekends or short vacations and flew home often to see my mother and friends in Stuttgart.

The opportunity to travel to distant lands and experience cultures made up for a rather frugal lifestyle while at home. My London experience was very different from my time in Paris. Having a full-time job, I did not stay out late at night or visit museums often. One time, though, I had an unforgettable experience: I had a ticket to the Royal Opera House Covent Garden to see Rudolf Nureyev and Dame Margot Fonteyn dancing. Oh, those leaps and beautiful movements! How my heart expanded! Ever since I was a little girl, I have loved ballet. My special treat as a teenager was to see the famous Stuttgart Ballet under John Cranko. I was very happy to be the watcher—my time to be the doer had not come yet. Making art myself was to come much later.

BRIGITTE BRÜGGEMANN | 53

My relationship with my boyfriend was less than ideal. I worked during the day, and he worked nights. We had very little time together, but somehow there was that vision of a future together. We became engaged just before he decided on another move to expand his career and hotel experience by accepting a job with an American hotel chain in the Bahamas. With a rather unclear idea about the when and how, we planned to meet back in Germany. I stayed in London for another year but felt lonely and isolated in England. I decided to move back to Stuttgart where I had friends and family.

It felt good to be home, living with my mother, giving her the support she so much deserved, giving back some for all her sacrifices raising us in hard times. Together, we found a small apartment for her to buy. It was a very good decision because she lived there by herself for thirty years until shortly after her hundredth birthday. It gave her the sense of independence and pride she had given up most of her life on behalf of her marriage and her children. She started to paint again, just as she had predicted years ago, after her children had left. Her caregiving was for herself now.

For me, back in Stuttgart, the future was a bit of a haze. W. kept extending his time abroad. I was in limbo having committed to a relationship but not living it. After a separation of two years, living very different lives, separated by an ocean and different cultures, we decided to try to be together. Throwing caution to the wind, I left my job in Germany and headed to Nassau in the Bahamas on a one-way ticket and a suitcase filled with hope and enthusiasm for life in an exotic environment.

CHAPTER 18

LIMBO ROCK

The Bahamians have a dance they often perform for tourists called limbo rock. The dancer, to the sound of steel drums and song, must bend over backwards, moving under a pole that is held lower and lower during the dance, challenging the strength and flexibility of the dancer. This, of course, is accompanied by the laughter and happy faces of viewers. Limbo rock was a perfect metaphor for what was ahead of me.

We had our wedding on the beach surrounded by my new husbands' coworkers and ex-pat friends. Despite the party mood under the palm trees, the steel drums, the blue sky, the sea, and the "yellow bird, up high in the banana tree"[2] (as the song goes), my wedding day was a lonely day for me far away from family members and close friends. But I was filled with excitement to live in a beautiful tropical environment and start a life with my beloved.

On the morning of my wedding day, I went to the beach to find white Plumeria flowers to make a wreath to wear in my hair. Later I walked down the aisle guided by a friend of my husband to be, a stranger to whom I had just been introduced. That special day was a combination of etiquette unfamiliar to me until I was handed a book on English customs by a caring new friend, and then following those rules of what was expected of a young bride. Smiling, I acted out my part in a movie. I had not realized that I could challenge those rules and walk down the aisle proudly by myself or on the arm of my new husband as is the custom in Germany.

I had given up the power to guide my destiny. I willingly surrendered myself to the idea of building a life together in this exotic environment, not asking for much in return. What had been familiar to me growing up—the role models of my father and mother—were a powerful influence; I had no other role models. Yet my deep-seated desire to find my path, my destiny, was a red thread woven into the tapestry of my life. It was always there, at times just a shadow, a reminder of who I was to become.

My husband was ambitious, working every day and often at night. His unavailability became familiar and acceptable to me. I would go out to the long stretches of white-sand beach, swimming, and snorkeling

---

[2] From the Song "Yellow Bird"—lyrics from a poem by Oswald Durand.

in the crystalline blue waters. I loved the underwater sea world until one day I was confronted by a barracuda. It was a dangerous encounter. I realized that being out there alone was not a good idea. I felt restless and limited by this exotic life of leisure. To be a wife and going to the beach every day did not give my life purpose. I was searching for what else was there.

In Europe, I had filled my free time looking at art, admiring the work of the masters. I had painted with watercolors but never felt "serious" about making art. I had not heard the call or believed in my ability to be good at it. Now I was removed from the influence of the masters in the museums. This deprivation, in a strange way, liberated me from being inhibited by thoughts of comparison and not being good enough. Now there was no judgment. My first set of oil paints was a Christmas gift. I playfully started to paint.

The colorful island culture of the Caribbean was exciting. I enjoyed the relaxed and fun-loving Bahamian people; the crystal-clear sea in jewel tones of blues, turquoise and greens; the white sandy beaches; the palm trees; and the blue skies. I wanted to capture some of this imagery and manifest a sense of life that was fresh air and sunshine. I had something that could give me joy and a meaningful way to pass my time in this new and different life. I found much pleasure going out to paint on a beach or picking some tropical flowers and paint what I saw.

I did not like to be dependent on my busy husband for everything. Against his wishes—"My wife does not work."—I started to look for a job. I had experience with the airlines and spoke several languages. Very quickly and without too much of an effort on my part, I was hired by a travel agency in Nassau, in the heart of town on Bay Street. I was surrounded daily by the tropical colorful hustle and bustle of the downtown area and the harbor, which was more real to me than a fancy hotel on Cable Beach. I loved the Bahamian people, their colorful clothes in purples, bright reds, yellows, and greens. I loved their big smiles under large straw hats. "Don't rush me, man" was a phrase I often heard. I loved the pink colonial architecture, the white shutters to keep out the hot sun, the lush tropical vegetation, and always the Caribbean Sea to frame the picture. There was always dancing to steel-drum music. It was all new and exciting; the work and the painting filled my days. I held on to that red thread in the tapestry, or maybe it was purple then?

"Island fever" came in after a while though. The small-island culture was focused on tourism—casino nightlife, lots of drinking, a life that after a while, somehow felt put on hold and superficial to me. My husband, in the pursuit of his professional career in hotel management, was offered a transfer with a working visa for both of us in the United States by an American hotel company. After two years in the Bahamas, we moved to the United States in 1971.

I was sleepwalking.

56 I GROWING WINGS

CHAPTER 19

LOSING MYSELF FOR A WHILE

We first arrived in the United States in Washington DC. This was followed by more moves from place to place as my husband climbed that corporate ladder. This corporate wife gave up looking for jobs. During those years, I was lost in the labyrinth of life. I spent the next twenty years trying to walk the middle of the road as my husband received promotions requiring us to move from city to city: Washington DC; Hartford, Connecticut; Houston, Texas; Memphis, Tennessee. It was all about his pursuit of the American Dream in corporate life. I had a different dream I did not remember.

Our daughter was born in 1972 in Connecticut. With joy, I gave myself totally to raising that amazing child with all my love. With Kim in the playpen next to me amusing herself by banging on pots and pans, I painted at the kitchen table. Soon I wanted to learn all I could about making art.

CHAPTER 20

GETTING CLOSER: MEMPHIS ACADEMY OF ART—1975

A major career move for my husband took us to Memphis, Tennessee, the headquarters of a large international hotel company. He was traveling in the corporate jet, and I was left to my own devices. There was not much communication between my husband and myself about what all that meant for me. I was a willing participant with the hope that there was something there waiting for me. Kim was three years old; I struggled with the responsibilities of a new mother in a strange city with no adult friends or family to consult with. Dr. Spock's *Common-Sense Book of Baby and Child Care* became my guide and helper.

Quote **Spock** emphasizes that ultimately, the parents' "natural loving care" for their children is most important. He reminds parents to have confidence in their abilities and to trust their common sense; his practice as a pediatrician had proven to him that parents' instincts were usually best. Unquote (Wikipedia)

We lived in an apartment complex with a pool. It was a place where I could meet people while Kim enjoyed playing in the baby pool. As serendipity had it, I met the young woman who lived next door. We talked about what we liked to do. She was a designer and saw my dilemma: I was feeling lost in an unfamiliar place with a small child and a desire for a creative outlet. The red thread showed up. Lynn helped me to get a part-time job I could do at home.

I was hired to paint her well-done pretty floral designs onto needlework canvases with templates to guide me. I learned and enjoyed mixing the paints exactly to match different colored yarns to be used in the needlework. The work gave me focus. I learned about colors and mixing pigments, a useful lesson I would rely on later. The project also gave me a sense of accomplishment as I was paid for each finished piece.

Eventually, we acquired our first house in the suburbs with a barbecue and a backyard, the American dream. We created our first garden from scratch after the construction rubble had been cleared. There was a beautiful flowering dogwood tree surrounded by azaleas and ferns. Our daughter had a backyard and neighborhood friends to play with, and we even had a litter of kittens. What an adventure! I loved decorating our first home, making drapes for the windows and paintings to hang on the walls. I was creating, I had a home now, but I often felt alienated by my own ethnocentricity. I heard comments about the way I dressed myself and Kim in "European style" recognizably different from the girly lacy pink and yellow clothing worn by American girls, or the synthetic color-coordinated women's outfits sold in the department stores. Little things were noticed by the neighbors as different and "strange" like our collection of clogs lined up by the back door, which was not a familiar sight at the time in the American South, but very normal and popular in Europe back then.

I felt more German than I would have living in Germany. I know that sort of thing is a fact for many people who live in foreign countries. A well-known German writer who lives in the United States, Ursula Hegi, wrote in her book, *Tearing the Silence* about living in theUnited States as a foreigner and how cultural stereotypes, being different, are instantly put onto the "immigrant."

I am also guilty of observing and judging differences. Most neighbors had station wagons for carpooling, a girl, a boy, and a dog. They made their purchases at Sears and went to church on Sundays. We had a VW Beatle, shopped wherever was convenient, had a small hibachi grill on the deck, and did not attend Sunday church. I tried to fit in and make friends, but when I talked to our neighbor about Germany or places I had been, she would say, "Oh, that's interesting." I knew she could not relate and was not interested in my stories of distant lands. I was looking into those windows again, observing people's lives from the outside.

I was filled with a yearning for more. Something was pulling on me, but I was not sure what it was exactly. I had started to paint again, experimenting with different styles and subjects, but I wanted help with ideas and decided to take some classes at the Memphis Academy of Art.

Kim was now old enough to go to daycare one day a week, I could go to class. Oh, I felt guilty dropping my little girl off at the nursery school, but in class, I completely took the time for myself. I loved the drawing and painting classes. My teacher inspired me with suggestions about imagery and abstraction. I was excited to create images that did not just illustrate what I saw in front of me.

I was very familiar with and had long loved the work of Kandinsky, the father of abstraction; Paul Klee; and the early twentieth-century European painters, but it had not occurred to me at the time to paint that way myself—to transcend what is there and paint the feelings that arise with what is there: paint from my emotional experience with a place or a situation. I could easily paint what I saw, but I wanted to learn how to listen to that inner voice. I had become numb to myself from the constant adjustments and tasks involved in resettling my family so many times.

My teacher noticed my commitment to painting and how easily it came to me. During one class, he suggested that I matriculate and become a full-time student. I was very surprised by his confidence in me. I said, "But I do not have a high school degree to study at a university or college!" I told him about my education in Germany, which did not qualify me for college in the United States. He said, "That's no problem. You can take the GED test and go to college." I also had a conversation with him about how I felt that I had nothing to say. There was that numbness again. He replied, "You will find that voice." I was shocked to see a door I could open, but I kept that idea hidden in my heart for six more years before I decided to take that General Education Development test and take the leap. I was, after all, in the "land of opportunity" that so many immigrants seek. Something was offered and was possible that would not have been in my path in Germany.

We had moved back to my hometown, Stuttgart, in Germany for a short stay in 1980. With great joy, I thought we had "come home" finally. My husband had realized what we had dreamed about—that he would become a hotel director in Germany. But after managing a large hotel in Stuttgart for just a few months, my husband decided to move back to the States for "better career opportunities." The original plan to live in Germany was abandoned; our original dream was tossed in the sea.

I did not agree with his decision. I considered not to go back to the States and, instead, staying with Kim in Germany. But I did not know—and dared not find out—how I would support myself. More importantly, I felt very strongly about Kim growing up with her father. I wanted to give her what I did not have as a child—to have a loving and supportive father who would be always present in her life.

Considering my options, I decided to find out what was there for me in the States. I was determined to find my calling. We moved back to Memphis, Tennessee and bought a lovely house to make me happy. I experienced a deep depression in that lovely house. I was searching for that red thread again, for the path forward. It started right there: next door. Our neighbor was a clay artist. She invited me to work with her. "Yes!" I said.

The work with clay was fun and very therapeutic for me. I learned to throw on the wheel and to hand build with clay, a meditative and centering process. I loved to get my hands into the clay; there was no thought, just form and earth. I shared a ceramic studio in the old schoolhouse of Germantown where we lived outside of Memphis. Serendipity was working for me again! I bought a kiln and started to work with children.

Behind our house was a school for behaviorally challenged teenage kids. I wandered into the campus one day for a visit. After speaking with the teachers about their work, I asked if I could work with the children once a week, hand building collaborative clay projects. "Yes!" they said.

I thought of a theme for the group and allowed each student to work on a part of the collaborative project with their own ideas. It was amazing to see those hyper kids calm down and work together. The work was therapeutic for the children and for me. I had unconsciously found a way to heal myself through working with others. Over time, I became centered again.

After just one year, without much regret on my part to leave the South, we moved again from Tennessee to Colorado, crossing another frontier—this time to the American Southwest.

CHAPTER 21

ART HAS ME NOW—COLORADO

Boulder, a short drive from Denver, became our new home. We had a view of the Front Range of the Rocky Mountains with large rock formations behind our house. It was a beautiful sight. The town was fun, with young energy, great weather, lots of outdoor activities like hiking and skiing. We had nice neighbors I could relate to. I felt refreshed and energized. We lived near the University of Colorado in Boulder, and I was back in the art department taking continuing education classes in drawing and painting.

Painting 101 was taught by a young graduate student. For our first still-life assignment, I painted the apples and bottles without much trouble; I took to paint like a fish to water, but I wanted to express something I did not even know what it was. I wanted to paint what I *felt* rather than what I *saw*. Deep in my heart, a door wanted to open so I could have a dialogue between my creative self and the painting.

My first large canvas was a leap of faith. It was an imaginary scene—a landscape of trees behind a garden fence with the gate open, inviting the viewer to walk into the space beyond. It was an abstraction of a landscape in nonobjective colors of pinks, and purples. Vertical shapes suggested trees and horizontal lines suggested distant mountains.

I was happy with this painting without realizing at the time that it was a metaphor for what I felt and what was to come for me: The gate in the painting (and in my life) was open, but there were obstacles and mountains to climb.

My teacher, whose abstract work was inspiring to me, quietly gave me support and encouragement to explore the possibilities of color, form, and content in a more abstract way. One day, he took some of the students' paintings to the faculty committee as examples of his students' work. He told me the faculty had been impressed with my painting. They suggested for me to enroll as full-time student. This was the second time I had been asked to matriculate. I could no longer ignore the call. I had to take the GED to become a full-time student seeking a degree in Fine Art.

The test was scheduled for a Saturday morning. I did not tell anyone to save myself the humiliation in case I did not pass. I had secretly studied for it and hoped to pass, but I had a plan B: If the university did not work out—if I did not pass that test—I was going to start a business making children's clothing. It was a way to keep myself from getting too attached to the results of the GED test.

Instead of going shopping that eventful Saturday, I took the test that would change my life. I mostly guessed the answers on the multiple-choice questions, choosing what seemed to be the most likely answer by elimination. What did I know about American history? How could I remember how to solve math problems twenty years after being in school? To my great surprise and great joy, I passed the test and could enroll in the arts program at the University of Colorado. I was going to college, the first woman in my family! I did not realize I was on my way to becoming an artist; I was going to study and learn lots of things.

CHAPTER 22

THE ART OF BECOMING

As a nine-year-old girl, I had stood in front of Matthias Grünewald's Isenheim Altarpiece in Colmar, Alsace Lorraine. I was awestruck by the work. I learned much later that the altarpiece had been commissioned in 1512 for the Antonine monks of the monastery at Isenheim. The monks were noted for their care of plague sufferers and their treatment of skin diseases. The image of the crucified Christ, his skin pitted with sores, showed viewers that Jesus suffered what they suffered. It was not so much the Christian imagery that touched me; it was the paint—what paint can do to evoke an emotional response. I knew then as a nine-year-old girl that, if a painting could touch my soul like that, painting was what I wanted to do.

Sometimes dreams take years to manifest. My dream had been to study art, learn how and what to paint, hold on to and follow that red thread in search for meaning in all those different places I had lived. I had found my way out of the labyrinth of life that felt limiting to me: I was growing my wings.

Journey,

pastel

BRIGITTE BRÜGGEMANN | 65

CHAPTER 23

UNDERGRADUATE YEARS

During my first year as an undergraduate, I often felt out of place as a "nontraditional student" among younger students, even though I had been used to feeling "out of place" for years, this was different because I wanted to fit in. I had just turned forty, a step into another phase of life. No longer being a "young person" brings uncertainty about the aging process and one's role in life. In hindsight, forty is young, so young. To walk on campus as a student was exhilarating for me. I could learn so many things and be challenged to walk new paths. My husband was tolerating, but not very supportive of my new experience. He would have preferred that I study business, that had been *his* ambition. I had decided on something different for myself. This was a first sign of our paths diverging.

In class I experienced some awkward moments. Once a young woman sitting next to me in an art history class asked me what I was doing there. Another time, as I walked into a room to take a test, I was told by someone at the door that the class was for students only. I had to adjust, find my way around campus. I wanted to fit in with the class, for a while, I tried to be invisible. I felt self-conscious and often apologized in a footnote in my papers for my English. I was afraid the first year to raise my hand in class to ask a question, thinking that my question was stupid. Then, when another student would ask that same question, I would be surprised. Eventually, I became more confident and was able to trust and follow my thoughts. Professors would leave notes in my papers telling me they loved "older students" and assuring me that my English was better than that of most students. My studio classes were a treat for me. I listened and learned and painted. I painted every minute I could spare.

The required classes for a liberal arts degree in science and humanities were challenging. I studied very hard for the exams, and to my surprise, made A's the first year and was on the dean's list with tuition waived. Slowly, I felt good about myself and my "right" to be there. However, four years later at my Bachelor of Fine Arts graduation ceremony, standing up with all the other students in my gown and cap, my blue graduating-with-honors ribbon pinned to my chest, self-consciously I looked around. I felt like an imposter. I thought, *is anyone going to find out that I do not deserve this?* I still did not trust myself.

The first two years of my undergraduate studies were mostly taken up by required studies for a liberal arts degree—science, humanities, and English. I was able to design my interdisciplinary program.

Science was not my strong point or interest, but I found classes that were interesting for me: geology, psychology, and anthropology, which covered the requirements for science.

Having read mostly German literature up to that point, I enjoyed the English literature classes. We studied works that ranged from Chaucer to Virginia Woolf and other contemporary women writers. Virginia Woolf's *"To the Lighthouse"* showed me a woman's perspective on society and relationships. May Sarton's *Journal of a Solitude* showed me how to live a solitary life as an artist, connecting to nature in a way that feeds the creative work. I was deeply touched by her poetic voice.

Women's studies opened a new understanding of my own experiences as a woman and inspired me to rethink how I wanted to live. With my eyes opened, I saw the injustice and chauvinism in our patriarchal culture and in my own experiences. I started to question much of what I had accepted as the role for a woman. Some of these insights were very personal and painful. I started to look at my marriage and saw things I wanted, things I could change, and things I could manifest for myself. I had been a young woman with independent ideas. I had traveled and sustained myself. I had given up my financial independence and what might have been different choices for love and marriage—the traditional path for a girl at that time. However, fortunately, all my experiences had led up to my becoming the artist I had dreamed of as a child. All my experiences came together in this opportunity. A seed had been planted and was sprouting. I yearned to have "a room of my own and £500 a year" (Virginia Woolf).

The studio classes were my passion. I put all the time I had into my studies, balancing my responsibilities as a wife and mother, taking care of my family and myself in the process. I felt as if I was on a rushing river that was taking me to the ocean.

Into the Ocean

pastel

It was challenging to be in two places at the same time—a wife and mother wanting to be there for the family, and the artist needing time and space for the emerging creative voice. At times it was difficult to keep going, to keep the fire burning in two places.

My years as an undergraduate student with a major in painting and drawing went by fast and was rich in experiences. I learned how to think and speak about art. I learned to understand what I saw. But not yet was I able to articulate what I wanted to say in my paintings; indeed, I didn't even quite know what it was I had to say. I took classes in painting, drawing, printmaking, and sculpture whenever I could find the time in my schedule.

Each semester I made sure I had time to drop Kim off at her junior high school in the morning on my way to class and pick her up in the afternoon to bring her home. I took care of the family before descending into the basement room to do my homework. Rarely did I go back to school in the evenings except for the visiting artist lectures by famous artists in all fields. I sat in the large auditorium watching the slides on the screen and listened to the artists. I felt one with it all.

I learned to believe in myself despite obstacles and question what the outcome would be. I had opened a door to that room of my own, to follow what I now knew was my calling. I was searching for my voice—what did I have to say with my paintings? Painting was not a hobby anymore; it had become central in my life.

I worked on two large paintings of human figures with wings. A narrative was emerging, yes, I wanted to fly. I was excited about those unfinished paintings They hung on the wall in my little corner of a studio in the art department under a staircase. Both paintings were stolen out of the studio one night. I was almost flattered, assuming the thief must have liked the paintings.

When I told my advisor about the theft, she said: "Why would anyone steal those paintings? They probably wanted them for the canvases." I was devastated that she saw it that way. I felt not at all supported by her throughout my studies. She was the only woman on the faculty at the time and may have been trying to toughen me up for a long and hard road ahead. I want to believe in her good intention here, but deep down I know differently. She probably saw me as the housewife who was dabbling in paint. She did not see *me*.

I had the support of several of my other professors but was always challenged and questioned about my intentions and what I wanted to say. That is the job of a professor. Teaching is not only about skills; it is almost more about challenging a student and bringing out the voice of a student. At times, this is a painful process.

During one critique, my painting professor questioned what I wanted the painting to say or "to be about." After my explanation, he said, "I do not get that." I projected my insecurity by interpreting that comment into, *I do not have the talent.* When I expressed that to him tearfully, he simply said, "If you did not have the talent, you would not be here." As painful as this moment was for me, it made me believe in myself. I am thankful for that moment in time. The studio is a solitary place; ten different critics have ten different opinions. Trust and clarity are needed to listen to that inner voice.

Determined to continue my studies, I applied and was accepted into the graduate program. I was given a studio on campus. Now I had much more time for intense studio work and independent study. The graduate art history lecture classes were focused on contemporary work, looking at what had been done in the *Zeitgeist* of this lifetime. It was helpful and necessary to know what other artists were thinking and doing. I was seriously searching for my voice as a painter.

My thesis show for my Master of Fine Art graduate degree was titled "Hours in the Garden." It did somewhat tie in with the historical genre women had been delegated to in the past. A woman chose or was told not to paint "important imagery" like battle scenes or other classic historical scenes but instead to paint pretty things—flowers, mother-and-child pictures, maybe portraits. That had been a women's place. Art history studies did highlight some exceptions, like courageous women painters in the Renaissance and early twentieth century who defied these boundaries. The New York School painters of the 1960s included some women, and the Women's Movement in the 1970s brought about works that challenged a woman's traditional place within genres. Art history (was his-story) textbooks until the 1980s included a sparse number of women painters; the big question is why? The role of women in society was changing; women became much more of a presence in Art.

For my thesis show, I created seven large organically shaped mystical garden panels that spoke of a "Paradise Lost." In twenty-four small paintings, I used wallpaper as a background. This was a subtle reference to the traditional domestic life of a woman. Wallpaper painted over with gestural abstract organic images spoke about "pattern" and my love for paint with luscious, free-spirited, loose brushstrokes.

The idea and imagery of patterns is often used in feminist work reflecting on women's lives, the patterns of care-taking and domestic tasks—the fabric of life. The regularity of daily tasks, multi-tasking, weaving together aspects of family life. Making it all work together like a tapestry was so much of my own experience too. In my work, I wanted to speak about the larger cycles of life, a desire for oneness instead of division and separation. Through the form, organic lyrical abstractions of vegetation, blossoms going to seed, light and dark, water and air, going beyond "flower painting," I was reaching for the content I wanted to speak about.

During my MFA oral exam, I sat in a circle with the professors of my committee surrounded by about forty of my paintings in a large, beautiful gallery space. A recording of bird songs played in the background, and the rich, sensuous, colorful images, organic abstractions, came together very well in an installation suggesting a garden-like environment: Hours in the Garden.

The challenging questions came up: Is beauty enough? Does this work go beyond the limitations of the flower painting genre? Is it more than an appeal to the senses? I had anticipated the questions. I was aware of the history of woman painters and the criticism of their work as pretty but not "important." I struggled for a good answer when one of my professors answered the question for me: "Yes, she proved that" he said: "beauty without apology." Ever since that moment, I do not apologize for beauty. I believe it touches and speaks to the highest energy, the divine in our hearts.

In my second year of graduate school, I experienced an epiphany, I realized I was an artist. It was a frightening "Oh, my God" experience! I saw the red thread, the path leading me into another life, a solitary life, to my "Journals of Solitude." To live the life of an artist had become a choiceless choice.

Silently I was asking for support on the journey on which I was about to embark. When the student is ready, the teacher will come; I remembered my family history.

My grandfather, around the turn of the twentieth century, was a well-respected guild master in the town of Reutlingen, Germany. He had studied at the Stuttgart Academy of Art and went on to a career in the decorative arts: fresco work, art deco design, gold leaf, painting murals, and faux finish work. His nine apprentices lived in my grandparents' house. My grandmother ran the household with an iron fist.

On weekends, grandfather would teach my mother, a teenager at the time, to paint. They went out into the countryside, sat by creeks and meadows, and painted. I have several of my mother's paintings. They are beautiful and accomplished. As a child, I looked at and touched her box of oil paints, brushes, and a wooden palette, hidden away in a drawer. I begged her to open it and show me, let me touch the brushes. She refused and said with a pained expression on her face, "When you all are grown and gone, I will start painting again." She did. Starting at age sixty-five, she painted beautiful abstract flower paintings in watercolor.

My grandfather also taught one of his apprentices who became a well-known painter in the region. My grandfather's work was lost when the house burned down, except for one little painting of a rose, which I treasure every day, and a lovely sketchbook that belonged to my grandfather, the work of—I think—one of his teachers. I loved to look at the egg tempera paintings in the book and the sketches of flowers and birds and bees. One little painting of a yellow bird on a branch with a farmhouse in the background was intriguing to me and was always one of my favorites in the book. The bird looks like a canary, a kind of surreal image as canaries usually are in a cage, not in the open fields.

Seeking support on my journey, I tried to connect with my grandfather's spirit. I never met him; he died years before I came into this world. I sought a connection to him on a mystical level asking for his support: "Stand behind me on this journey."

One day in my garden, a yellow canary-like bird sat on a branch looking at me as if he had just flown out from my grandfather's sketchbook. I reached out to him, and to my great surprise, he flew onto my finger! I thought it was someone's pet bird that had got away. I took him into the house and let him fly around one bedroom with the door closed to keep him safe from my cats. A neighbor took the bird to the animal rescue shelter where she was working. She told me later they had checked the bird out and found that he was a wild bird after all. I have no explanation for this story. It was magical for me to have a wild bird sitting on my finger. I felt my grandfather had shown himself to me in the body of the yellow bird from his sketchbook. Grandfather has been with me in the studio in spirit many times since that day.

Yellow Bird

encaustic/collage

CHAPTER 24

SIGNS AND WONDERS

After receiving my MFA, I realized that possibly I could support myself with my art and teaching! I was headed into crisis. It was decision time: I would have to leave my world of twenty years as a corporate wife if I decided that I could not just be the Sunday painter my husband wanted me to be. He demanded my full attention as a wife. To leave my family was frightening and painful. I had become very serious to walk my walk; there was no choice anymore to be or not to be an artist.

Events and people came into my life, catalysts that made me see my relationship in a different light and that helped me see that it was time to make that huge decision—to ask for a divorce.

Through shamanic work, I found my connection to the spiritual energy that helped me make decisions and find answers to many questions. One day when I was hiking in the mountains thinking about what to do, how to navigate this passage, I heard a voice coming out of a dead tree: *We will take care of you.*

It was a real voice, an actual voice with no one there coming out of that dead tree. I shared this experience with a fellow graduate student, Michael. He chuckled and explained about other non-ordinary realities. He taught me the way of the shaman through drumming and journeying to find guidance and help from my guardian spirits. I kept on listening and asking questions, watching for signs and symbols. I had taken another step on the journey. I lived on my own, liberated to make my own decisions, but running out of money. I was too proud to ask for support from my husband; after all, I decided to leave and achieve independence.

I decided to scan the horizon for a teaching job. One day, as I was looking at the daily job listings in the paper, I saw an advertisement for a front desk job at a large chain hotel. I knew some things about the hotel business, and I spoke three languages. During the interview I was told that it was the practice of the company to hire front desk personnel by promoting from within. (This is not what the ad had suggested.) I had to start as a housekeeper—as a maid—making up beds and cleaning toilets. The irony was that my husband was a high executive in another large international hotel chain. Because I needed a job, I agreed to do the "training." They sat me down in a basement room with a tutorial video about housekeeping.

While I was watching how to make a bed and clean a toilet, I felt more and more desperate. I realized how exhausting and demoralizing this job would be, emotionally and physically. Would I still find the energy to paint? I left the basement room without telling anyone, even before the video was finished.

As I drove home, I questioned myself: How stupid was I to let this one job go? Interviewers for other jobs for which I had applied all said the same thing: "You are over-qualified and will leave as soon as you find something better." This was probably true. I was tired and feeling very low when I put the key into my apartment door and heard the phone ringing inside. It was the woman in charge of the University of Colorado continuing education program calling to offer me a teaching job. I had made a proposal to the program a few weeks earlier. The woman told me that she was impressed by my story because I had started as a continuing education student and then worked through undergraduate and graduate school. She wanted to give me a chance because that was what continuing education was about—the nontraditional student going back to school to learn a new skill. I was going to be a part-time adjunct professor, teaching painting 101 in the same studio in which I had started my first painting class as a continuing education student.

This mysterious series of events taught me about the power of intention: I had turned down a meaningless job to keep my energy and time open for what I wanted. Signs and wonders.

CHAPTER 25

TRUST

For several years, I struggled financially. Besides the teaching job, I worked other part-time jobs during the day to support myself, but I always kept my focus on doing my work—making art.

I lived in a small apartment with a loft that I used as my studio. Driven to express what had been held back for so long, I worked every free minute, sometimes late into the night. Since I could not use oils in the apartment because of the turpentine fumes, I discovered pastel work as a good and fairly nontoxic media. Because I was able to work quickly, the imagery came through in magical, alchemic ways. I often wondered where the image was coming from. I had opened the door for inspiration, for the muses to speak through me.

I found a gallery in Denver and in Boulder that showed my work and worked part-time in a gallery. One day I met a woman in the gallery who wanted to share her studio. She had just moved to Boulder from New York and was suffering from a deep depression. Her paintings were dark and muddy. If I shared her studio, I could work in oils again. My work was about color and light. Even though I was experiencing challenging life changes, my escape from anxiety, fear, and the pain of divorce was bringing color and light into my life through my paintings. It was therapeutic for Cindy to see my work next to her in the studio. She started to allow the light to come into her heart and soul, and her paintings became colorful and very beautiful.

By teaching night classes at the university, working part-time at the gallery, and selling bedding plants at the local hardware store, I was able to just get by, painting when I could at night. As I lived outside of my comfort zone, I was reaching for spiritual support through my shamanic work, and the struggle gave me much to speak about in my paintings.

My first big sale of work in the Boulder gallery came through. I sold twelve pastels to an architect in Denver who was designing an office building in Boulder and was looking for art to grace the lobby. He bought twelve paintings, my first big sale! The money from the sale enabled me to take some time off in the summer to travel for the first time to New Mexico. Through an ad in the newspaper, I found a retreat center north of Taos in need of a work-study. Once again, I was moved along my path in mysterious ways.

The summer program of the retreat center was based on Native American teachings, which I knew nothing about. When the Lakota Sioux medicine man arrived to hold sweat lodges and share his teachings, he spoke much about the "red road," the path the Lakota Sioux follow on their spiritual journey. For me it had been the "red thread" in the tapestry of my life that I followed. I cried for days—tears of healing and letting go. Whenever I felt overwhelmed with grief and fear of the unknown, I picked up a broom and swept the floor. It helped me sweep fearful thoughts from my mind.

I loved New Mexico—the open sky, the vast expansive land, the medicinal sagebrush, the hiking trails in the mountains near Taos. I lived in a small rustic cabin surrounded by sagebrush. I set up my drawing table outside in the open with the sky above, eagles and hawks circling, and the Sangre de Cristo Mountains looking down on me. As above so below, I created a portfolio that turned out to be very successful in the galleries.

The summer gave me distance and time to think about my future and find balance. I wanted to leave Boulder with its many memories and attachments. I wanted to start a new life. With that realization, I needed to get a full-time teaching position. I wrote to universities in California, Colorado, and New Mexico to see, if by chance, I might have missed a position advertised in the journals for higher education.

Some of my letters were never answered, some were answered with regrets. Two colleges encouraged me to apply for positions that had not been advertised nationally. I applied to Highlands University of New Mexico in Las Vegas, New Mexico, and the Fresno City College, in California. I was asked by both for an interview. I was turned down for the Fresno position but was offered a tenure track job as Assistant Professor of Art to teach painting and drawing at Highlands University in Las Vegas, New Mexico.

I was grateful to land that job out of many applicants, but my feeling about the town was very mixed. I had lived in major cities like Paris and London, and here I was in a very conservative small town in a rural community that seemed to be stuck in the past. I brushed my concerns aside because I needed that safety blanket of a job. I did not believe yet that I would be able to make a livelihood from just the sale of my work. I was excited to be able to sustain myself with what I loved to do—teach art, passing on the information I had been taught and what I had found out for myself in the studio. I was eager to help students to see, experience, and make art, guide them to find their voice, and answer the question that I had asked myself: What do I have to say and how will I say it?

BRIGITTE BRÜGGEMANN | 77

CHAPTER 26

TEACHING: LAS VEGAS, NM—1990

A full-time, tenure-track position in New Mexico was waiting for me. I had a difficult tearful good-bye with my daughter, who was heading for college in Santa Barbara, California. My husband and I, after a twenty-year marriage were now also on our own.

I climbed into my rented eighteen-foot U-Haul truck with a very heavy heart to drive myself and my belongings to New Mexico. I had never driven a large truck before, but I got on the interstate and made it to New Mexico without major problems, except having difficulty backing up in a gas station, an effort I accomplished finally with some anxiety based on fear. I drove down a narrow back road to my new home, the main road having been flooded out after recent monsoon rains. Friends from Boulder were helping me to move and had been driving behind me. They told me with grins on their faces that had I missed hitting a large rock formation on one side of the road by a few inches. On top of that rock was a large statue of Christ blessing what was below!

The university was running a low budget in the art department. Enrollment was low for art; the department had been red flagged. At first, I did not understand how serious that was. All the previous art faculty members had left what they probably thought was a sinking ship.

The faculty members in the department were newly hired. One colleague taught sculpture and foundry, a part-time colleague taught printmaking, and I taught painting and drawing. The administration expected professors in the art department to teach, teach, and teach—five days a week. The university had been founded as a teachers' college and operated under a different approach from that of the research university I was coming from. This was a problem in the making for me: an artist teaches from his or her experience with studio work for ongoing exhibitions of their work, which takes time outside of teaching.

Physical studio spaces and the lecture hall were in terrible shape and lacking equipment. Imagine a painting studio without natural light, students working with turpentine without ventilation or windows to open, tables and easels dirty and uncared for. But, for lack of other options, I accepted the challenge of what was offered with cheerfulness, a positive approach, and much energy.

Over the next five years, my colleagues and I redesigned the program with much enthusiasm. The enrollment improved dramatically. We added more classes in all disciplines and fixed up the studio spaces and equipment. I focused on fleshing out the drawing and painting program, which was my responsibility. What was new for me was teaching a course called Introduction to Art, an art history lecture class. Even though I had studied art history extensively, I had to prepare the lectures for a class of a hundred students.

I was familiar and comfortable with the studio classes, but I truly had to gather up all my knowledge and courage to teach a lecture class. My introduction to the course started with reading the roll call. I butchered the students' Spanish names, getting chuckles and moans in response. I looked up from the list and, with a smile, asked the students to pronounce my name. This broke the ice, made them smile and understand. As I projected slides onto the screen in a darkened room, the images of the beloved masterpieces helped me tremendously to overcome my inhibitions. My excitement for the work enabled me to speak freely, my words and thoughts were backed up by my knowledge of the many works which I had seen in Museums during my travels.

Immediately, in my first-semester offerings, I added a life drawing class, a foundation class for drawing with life models. I was called into my department chair's office. To my great amazement and distress, I was told that there had never been a life drawing class in the program because it was considered "problematic" in the small conservative town to use nude models. In my first week of school, I was ready to quit unless I could teach that essential foundation studio class. My chair agreed with great hesitation but requested I did not use locals as models.

An even bigger problem was to get the students, who came from conservative backgrounds, to be okay with nude models. I remembered my own first life drawing class back in Memphis, Tennessee, and how I'd had to find a way to get over my inhibitions. I simply stayed focused, worked fast with intensity, got out of my head, and make that connection from my eyes to my hand that held the drawing tool. After the initial adjustment, students were fine and started to see the human figure as a challenge different from drawing still lives, to see form and shapes in relationship to each other quickly and to capture the emotional quality of movement with gestural line work.

One day early in the semester, a husband stormed into the studio during a life drawing session and ordered his wife to leave the class. She left with him but showed up for the next class. I guess she had a good talk with her husband about what she wanted to do. She turned out to be a very good student and graduated with a BFA years later.

BRIGITTE BRÜGGEMANN | 79

Drawing classes went well. I had a lot of fun with the students. I started each class by smudging the room with sage and conducting a short meditation to get the students coming in from other lecture classes centered and quiet. These were new and unfamiliar practices for many students. The smell of the sage had professors in the lecture hall next door think we were smoking grass! One student, confused about meditation at first, told me later she grew to love the practice.

My two faculty colleagues also expanded the sculpture, printmaking, and art history curricula. A foundry, which was not offered at many other university art departments in the state, was built. It became a real attraction to students, mainly, I think, because of the hands-on process of foundry work and the job opportunities with commercial foundries in a state where many artists live and work. Pretty soon the program grew in enrollment, and we were able to hire part-time instructors to cover additional classes. We received accreditation for a BFA, a bachelor's degree in fine art, which attracted serious art students to the school.

With all that was going on for me, I missed my family. My daughter was in college in California going through the adjustment of being on her own. I tried to see her as often I could, and we talked on the phone. She had a difficult time with the divorce, but over time, her new life in a beautiful spot in California made her strong and self-sufficient. My ex-husband and I stayed good friends and visited occasionally. There were still aspects of our lives to share. We all had to re-invent ourselves.

I lived in a lovely little house by a creek with a small studio in which I spent all my free time. My work sold at galleries in Denver, Boulder, Aspen, and Houston, with solo shows every year. I was busy and grateful. The house was near the United World College in Montezuma, New Mexico, outside of Las Vegas, a refreshing environment that attracted young students from all over the world. The college was sponsored by Arm and Hammer and was part of the United World Colleges located in every United Nations member country. The mission was to foster peace and understanding between nations. Young, talented people are chosen from the brightest and most promising of their country. They live and learn together for two years before going back to their home countries with baccalaureates, ready to go to college. I lived next door to the campus, met the students and faculty often, made friends, and took part in some of the activities on campus. One of the faculty members, an artist, became my very good friend, he was like a brother to me. We talked often about art and life and still today are good friends.

Even with my busy schedule at the college and doing my studio work for exhibitions, I was often lonely for companionship, but I put these feelings aside. I somehow knew that, in my experiences with romantic partners, I was too willing to give up my priorities. I often found myself giving up what is most important to me—my work—to make space for a relationship.

This, in my experience, is not usually an issue for the man when the tables are turned. A man's work is *his* work, and his woman "should" be at his side. When I was involved with my work—all aspects of it including the making and the marketing—I often heard "You have no more time for me. I am losing you to your business." This is not just my experience. There are other women artists, famous artists, wives of famous artists, who have given up their work for a time to be of service to their families and their husbands' careers.

CHAPTER 27

FINDING MY PLACE—TWO YEARS LATER

When I was still living in Boulder, Colorado, I had a vision during a shamanic journey: I was in a canoe on a river. In the helm of the boat in front of me sat a big white polar bear navigating around the rocks in the river. To the right of us was a steep slope with sparse vegetation, red earth, and large boulders. To the left was a meadow. I did not recognize this landscape of red, stony, arid earth. The bear pulled the boat over to the bank. I climbed out to walk over the meadow, which was covered with scattered grasses and patches of small white daisies. One large, majestic oak tree stood as if to protect the space. Behind the oak, a gentle upward slope was covered with juniper trees. I felt great joy. I had come home. I asked: is this a real place? I knew that it may be, or it may be just a place in my heart.

After I had moved to New Mexico, I wanted to find "a place of my own." I drove around different areas on weekends to look for a house or land for sale that could work for me, but I was not clear what I was looking for; I only knew I wanted a studio and solitude.

I met with a real estate agent. Behind him as he sat at his desk was a painting of an Indian sitting on a rock ledge overlooking a river. The agent asked me what I had in mind. Without thinking, I said I would like to be near water. I was rather surprised to hear myself say this. (I realized the challenge; there is not much water in New Mexico's high desert.) The agent looked at me with curiosity and said, "As a matter of fact, I have just listed a property on the Pecos River. I will show it to you." The next day, we drove down an almost nonexistent dirt road that wound among arid hillsides, juniper trees, cactus plants, and rocks. When I got out of the car near an overlook, I heard the river rushing below, and I saw a horizontal large red rock formation across the river with a dip as if a giant hand had pushed it down toward the river, to me a mark of energy moving. Below, the river was a silver ribbon that meandered between the juniper trees. I stood, not quite understanding what I saw. At my feet lay a small, flat heart-shaped rock covered with lichen. I picked it up and held it while we walked the land and the adjoining meadows along the river.

The agent, instead of a sales pitch, told me in a patronizing voice, "There are problems with this land. There's an old access issue. There is no infrastructure—no road, no water, no electric. You, as a single woman, do not want to deal with this raw piece of undeveloped land." We walked along the river toward an old apple orchard and a broken-down homestead. I turned around and looked up toward the outcrop where I had found the heart-shaped rock. I understood then that this was the land I had been shown in my shamanic vision years earlier. This was to be my home.

I took some time to act on this strange coincidence, the manifestation of a vision, of a dream. The next week I had to go to Boulder for the opening of my show in a gallery. It was a blessing to have some time and space between me and the magic opportunity. I wanted to be sure of my actions. I had no one to consult with but myself. I made an offer on the land, I contracted for a road to be built, brought in a power line, and found water. It all happened easily without any stress. It was meant to be. I had never done anything like that before in my life. I took it step by step, seeking out information and making decisions with caution.

When workers were drilling for the well, I drove down the road after work to see if they had struck water yet. A beautiful white stallion came running up the road toward me, his mane and tail flying in the wind catching the sunlight. I saw it as a message of power and support. At the site, water was gushing up in a huge fountain. I had water! I could live here!

Next, I had to find a builder. I happened to visit an open house on a Sunday in a subdivision of Santa Fe. I liked the way the house felt and the quality of the workmanship. I talked with the builder on the site and asked him if he was at all interested in building out in the country near San Isidro, the village close by. He looked at me, amused, and told me that he was planning to build two houses out there on land that someone had traded with him to settle a debt. He said that, if I decided on the floorplan which he was planning to do there, he could build me a house on a budget that would work for me. I looked at the model house he had built in a contemporary territorial style with a pitched roof that I liked. It had a functional open floor plan with high ceilings in places. I had a builder! Magic was working again!

We worked well together. He was honest and supportive. The foreman and crew for the project lived out near the site as well. Some people gave me warnings: "You'd better get a good lawyer." One of my students gave me a book to read: *Building a House Without Stress*. The main message was: decide that you will have fun with this, be cautious in your decisions, be involved, and be determined to have a positive experience. And so it was.

While my house was being built, I lived in Santa Fe in a little apartment. The space was very tight, but I could paint in the second bedroom. I commuted every day two hours to teach in Las Vegas but being in town provided an opportunity for me to be close to friends on weekends and do fun things when I was not painting. It was an exciting time filled with joyful anticipation mixed in with stress that comes with financial commitments and my budget limitations. I survived occasional anxiety attacks by pummeling a pillow!

On Saturdays I joined an African dance class in the arts district known as the Railyard. It was empowering to move my body to the drums; the energy in the room was great and contagious. I had not experienced a feeling of energy flowing freely in my body in a no-mind state like that before. After dancing I would visit the farmers' market for fresh produce, enjoying the people, the music, and activities there before going back to my solitary life.

House on the Hill

watercolor

JOURNAL ENTRIES

Journaling is a morning ritual for me to center myself and focus on the moment. I write down what I hear, what I see, what I feel. In my solitary life, it is a way to enter a dialogue with something outside of myself. It gives me peace and solace. The inner voice speaks in these writings.

June 21st Solstice

I danced again today; how good it makes me feel! I forget dark thoughts, fear, and desires. When I move to the sexy rhythm of the drums, I am in the moment. I do not want anything more than this moment of bliss. In the following days, I lose that carefree way again until the next time I dance. Dancing without your feet is the real assignment—every day and every moment.

Solitude can turn into loneliness. I am watching my thoughts. The heart speaks loudly to turn loneliness into blessed aloneness. That is my wish. I send my prayers to the clouds, the sky, and whoever wants to listen, out beyond that great field.

Springtime—the garden is so very beautiful. The devas, the garden spirits are here. I had my first meal from the garden—fresh snow peas and some rice, a few sweet peppers, some tomatoes. I am grateful for that meal.

I finished—for the fourth time I think—a commissioned painting. The process gets interesting when a patron is involved: the dialogue with the painting gets muddled. It is wonderful for people to believe in my work enough to trust it will be what they want to live with. For me it is a bit of a catch twenty-two: I want to please and make it right, but I also need to allow for the unfolding. The client who commissioned this painting wanted something changed and then wanted me to take it back to the way it was. That cannot happen, it can only move forward, and it did. It is done. In the process, I was gifted by another small painting that happened in a second while I cleared my thoughts. I am very happy. It was a long time in coming—an easy painting, a gift from the gods. I might call it that.

Today I had a bad day and night with my right hand. Suddenly I was struck with an unexplainable pain in my middle finger—arthritis. I have done too much with that hand—planting, hauling rocks, building rock walls. I am getting older. I realize this when I look in the mirror. But then again, on some days I have a brilliant energy field around me. On that thought, good night.

CHAPTER 28

PAINTER OF LIGHT

During a visit to Munich to see my family, I went to the Old Pinakothek to see the overwhelming collection of paintings by many old masters. My preference has always been to focus on a few artists each time I go into a museum. I visit a few of the paintings and stay with them for a while. I was on my way through various rooms to see a specific painter—Vermeer, a painter of light. Turning a corner in the Flemish section, I came upon the work of Jan Breughel the Elder. There on the wall was a favorite still life: "Flowers in a Wooden Vase." He had painted a bouquet of flowers that do not bloom at the same time of year. From early first-spring flowers to late roses, all were arranged in a vase together. The cycle of life was also suggested with overripe rotting fruit and little bugs crawling on the table.

I have always loved the subtle comment on life and death in those still-life paintings, a Vanitas painting, a genre of paintings that alludes to the vanity of worldly pleasures and life's transient nature. I looked at every beautiful detail—the coloration and blending of colors, the transparency of the flower petals, the contrast between the background to foreground, the light and dark, the light reflecting on the wing of the little bug crawling on the tablecloth, the masterful composition moving my eye around the painting from one flower to the next. The painting was alive and filled me with appreciation and joy for the beauty and the ephemeral voice I heard about life and death. I was inspired.

Back home, I stretched a large canvas and started painting at night in my crowded little apartment. I used acrylics to avoid the turpentine fumes and painted with my fingers at times, spreading and smoothing the paint into layers.

In my own Vanitas painting brilliant red areas suggest blossoms. Dark swooping clouds are next to misty whites and suggestions of blue, all abstract forms. Not sure yet if the painting was finished, I woke up one night to have a look at it. I sat there in the dark room, except for the spotlight on the painting and started to weep. Looking at the painting, I saw my own mortality in time. I realized that, in our lives, we waste so much time with things that do not move us forward along our path.

Vanitas

acrylic painting

CHAPTER 29

THE KISS OF THE HUMMINGBIRD

I had just finished a painting inspired by the colors in my garden: a pink oleander bush right next to a bright orange trumpet vine that graced my studio window. The hummingbirds had visited these flowers all summer long. Their joy was also mine. The colors of the flowers found their way into the painting.

After I decided on the title, honoring the hummingbirds, my little friends during the summertime, I went outside to sit on a wall in the sun in a meditative state of no mind. A hummingbird came up to me and hovered behind me for a while as if he was gathering courage, dashed away, came back to peck me on my cheek with his long beak, hurried away again, as if embarrassed, not looking back. I took it as a sign of approval.

De-light of the Hummingbird

oil painting

CHAPTER 30
BUILDING A PAINTER'S DREAM

A Lakota Sioux women friend came out to my land before the construction of my house started. Overlooking the valley, she drummed and chanted, asking for help to have this project go well. Considering the violent history of this part of the country—Indian country conquered by the conquistadores. I asked a Lakota Sioux medicine man who lived close by to clear the energy of the land and to bless my new home.

After the foundation of the house was staked out, I smudged the circumference with sage. With a smoking smudge stick, I came to where the front door was to be. As I bent down to smudge the imaginary threshold, a bee buzzed around me and stung my hand. It did not hurt much, but the bee gave her life with the sting. I always have seen the bee as a sign of the goddess; I took the sting as her blessing.

During this time of construction and after, I had some experiences with male neighbors "crossing my boundaries" with actions that were not only rude and thoughtless but showed chauvinistic entitlement and disrespect. I was rather amused when I realized that I was perceived to be "unusual" for a woman. At a meeting with future neighbors to decide on the planning of a road, the mother of one neighbor asked me with disdain what I was doing there by myself without a man. Another neighbor told me I should smile more. As a single woman, I had learned to be firm, clear and to stand my ground. Often the responses I received were patronizing, masochistic, aggressive, even abusive as I was told to go back to where I had come from. I did see the possible harm I put myself in. I did not always make friends. I became a hermit.

Helen Reddy's song spoke to me and encouraged me in many ways to follow that red thread:

> I am woman …
>
> You can bend but never break me
>
> 'Cause it only serves to make me
>
> More determined to achieve my final goal
>
> And I come back even stronger

Not a novice any longer

'Cause you've deepened the conviction in my soul.[3]

Here, on this river of my dreams, I can heal, follow the breadcrumbs put out to me in the forest of life, confront my fears, and follow my "inner necessity." I can do the work that is precious to me. I can find peace by the river of dreams.

A Painter's Dream

pastel

---

[3] From the song "I Am Woman"—written by Helen Reddy ad Ray Burton.

CONVERSATIONS:

Water Fire Stone.

I am water flowing ever new,

rushing dark taking everything with me.

I am slow running quietly,

singing my song.

I carry colored leaves

into eddies round and round in backwaters.

Suddenly I find a way out

into the mainstream.

I am fire, smoke,

blaze, hungry, I consume anything,

burn skin and eyes, green poison smoke,

dancing flames—orange, purple.

I also warm cold feet and hands,

nurture sister earth with my ashes,

bodies of coal guardians.

I am stone,

ancient, solid, unmoving witness to ages,

hard emotions.

I sharpen the knife.

I wait for the rains

to roll me down the bank into the water.

Fire and ice on the river.

Frost tonight. The water in the hummingbird feeder is frozen. The little birds are confused. Do they understand the change from a liquid into solid mass?

Things change so quickly from a state of flux into one of density; liquid water takes on any form or shape of the vessel it is contained in. The ice cannot change or adjust its form until it is melted by the sun again.

I look at the human condition and, using the metaphor of water and ice, I understand. How often have I felt that frozen state: unmoving, accepting the way things are, fitting into and staying with that form. And then: here comes the sun melting everything to a fluid state again. Everything flows and moves. What about water evaporating? Is that where we go eventually? Free from form and boundaries?

The rain, like solitude, comes from the ocean and goes back to it. Last night—thunder and lightning passed over my roof. Aahh, what a beautiful sound. I will start that new painting today.

In the silence of this morning, cool, fresh air before the heat, my morning ritual begins, a precious time each day. I sit outside with my coffee, let my eyes wander without focus from tree to flower to cloud, I listen to the birds, and feel the happiness and stillness inside and around me. I know I will have a good day if I can maintain being centered without hopes and desire. With this very thought, expectation sneaks in, taking the stillness away.

There, on the little gate into the arroyo, a large bird jumps up gracefully like a gymnast, whipping his long tail. A rather large bird. A pheasant? No, it is a roadrunner. He jumps off—again whipping his tail—and then majestically, placing each step with such dignity, walks along the little stone wall and disappears behind a bush. Then he is gone. I heard they are hunting snakes. Good hunting!

Later,

I hear a knock on my glass door.

The roadrunner holds a lizard in his beak,

knocks, looks in.

He wants to give me the lizard.

I say thank you, and he hops away.

Another day he came with a snake.

I looked at him. He looked at me,

moving his long tail in a circular fashion

with eye contact. I talked to him through the window.

Then he ran away whipping his tail up and down.

Farewell to summertime.

I am working the garden today

much to do before the winter

gathering leaves

cutting the grassy clover patch

trimming and transplanting

I bring in some of the plants

to live in the little studio for the next month

I still feel the sun on my back

the rain clouds have a rendezvous in the sky

rain starts, stops and starts up again

I could get nostalgic

summer is gone

winter is coming cold and hostile

at least from this vantage point

listen to the bird sing

a song of gratitude I want to learn from them

a grasshopper leaps to find another meal

plants are going to seed

I sense richness in this moment of closure

I stop to take notice of the change

I can see the color of the leaves change as I look

a few hours ago still green now they are yellow

I plant some pretty tulips something to put to bed

I can wake up in a few months adoring the pretty colored tulips

dream time—I make a fire inside

Blackfoot my cat happily settles down on his favorite chair

stretches out in front of the woodstove with gratitude—

the best place to be in the next few months

farewell summertime when the living is easy.

PART 3
MAKING IT WORK

CHAPTER 31

PAINTING IS THE WORK

Teaching was a "safety blanket." I know about myself that too much comfort makes me lazy. I had not reached out for local representation; neither did I have enough time to work every day in the studio. I knew that I would eventually have to get out from under that blanket that was keeping me too comfortable and did not get the work out enough.

I was passionate about teaching. Most of our students had grown up in the local rural conservative community and had had very little exposure to Fine Art. We had some difficult critiques; I was frustrated by the limitations of the students' knowledge of art history; their limited creative ambitions; and their lack of self-esteem, trust, and curiosity. I tried to be supportive of where they were, and, at the same time, introduce them to the unfamiliar and the creative part of themselves.

It took much of my energy and time to teach in an environment that was not supportive of my own studio work. Teaching was what I was hired for. I had started to sell my work at galleries in Colorado, Denver, Boulder, Aspen, and Vail, and in Houston, Texas. To have several galleries representing me meant that I had to produce work for exhibitions, but my time was limited by teaching 5 days a week.

I did not quite believe in what seemed the impossible dream: making a livelihood from my work only. The "starving artist" idea was still with me from that early experience when I was sixteen and thinking about a creative career path. If I wanted to make a living from my work without relying on my income from teaching, I had to ask myself some questions, make another plan B, fend off the fear.

I had developed a style and imagery in my pastel drawings that sold well. But the sales from the works on paper was not enough to sustain me. Works on canvas fetch a much higher price in general than works on paper. Something about my canvases needed to change so they would appeal to collectors. Maybe there was a way to not be the starving artist? Many artists make a living from their work. I had seen the red dots that indicated sales of paintings in the galleries. I was seeking something authentic in my canvases, an aspect of beauty that would speak to what might be a more selective audience with an eye for the abstract, less familiar, less recognizable imagery. That was my work; that was my intention. I needed more time to look at my options.

CHAPTER 32

STRETCHING MY WINGS

Teaching at the university gave me a nice, long summer break from the middle of May to the middle of August. I needed a break from the intense first years of teaching and adjustment to a different environment and culture. I needed to clear my head.

I decided to take a major trip by myself after many years of family travel. It was a big decision, made on the spur of the moment: I wanted to see and feel Bali. I had read about the Mother Mountain—Mount Agung—on Bali, an active volcano. I had read about the Balinese people, who feel a responsibility to balance the Universe with their rituals. I knew about the dances, I wanted to experience that exotic island, and booked a ticket. I would have to figure out everything when I got there.

After a long flight out of Los Angeles, I landed in Hawaii. After sixteen additional nonstop hours, I arrived in Denpasar, found my way into Ubud and to a hotel recommended by the Taxi driver. In the morning, I woke up to a cacophony of tropical sounds—birds crowing and cawing in the trees. The air was humid, the vegetation was dense., amazing, beautiful, tropical and inspiring. Uncertainty about what I would find had melted to allow for a beautiful adventure. I took long walks, admired the little shrines in every rice paddy, the temples, the dances, the food, the beautiful people. Every day a graceful young woman left a little tray of woven palm leaves, a flower, a shell, burning incense, a blessing and offering on my front porch.

One day, I walked and walked until my hip started hurting. I had never experienced that pain before, I was bewildered and just sat on some steps in front of a shop to rest. Across the street was a small restaurant that looked very inviting. I knocked at the heavy carved wooden door. A beautiful, young, smiling Balinese man, his black hair tumbling down his back, ushered me in. He asked where I was from, not an unusual question for a tourist in Bali. He smiled even more and led me to a low table to share with three German women who were already sitting there, sketching the scenery. A soft breeze gently moved the bright green leaves in the rice paddies that bordered the restaurant.

I had an instant connection with one of the women. We became friends and traveled around the island together. She had once been a teacher in Tübingen, a little town near Stuttgart I knew well. She was a disciple of Osho and lived near the Ashram in Poona, India. She shared her story of addiction and her journey that had led her to Osho's Ashram in India. We sat on the beach listening to a tape, one of Oshos' teachings about love. I was deeply touched; he cracked open my heart that very moment.

After coming back home from Bali, I felt refreshed and energized again, ready for another semester. A series of juicy pastel drawings came to me, inspired by the sights I had seen—lush vegetation, temple architecture, rich textures everywhere, and the joy of life. The series sold very quickly and gave me the confidence I needed for the next step.

CHAPTER 33

INTO THE UNKNOWN

After five years of teaching, I came up for tenure, it was decision time for me: should I stay with what is save but stressful, or should I find "that other way" to support myself? There was tension in the department, not un-typical for academia; I wanted to live without stress. I decided not to apply for tenure, and with that decision, I threw off that safety blanket. Without the security of tenure, there would be no more paychecks to count on in a few months. I wanted to at least try to make a livelihood from my art against all predictions. How would I know I could not do it if I did not try?

Fear still held its place in my mind. I was worried about my future; in three months, I would have no steady income. I had a mortgage and was terrified of losing my house. But my priority was to balance my energy and heal myself from teaching in a rather unsupportive environment. I had severe tendonitis in my shoulder, it was a manifestation and my unconscious way of holding on to security, that safety blanket, it was making me sick. I needed to let go and find a way forward. A health situation in my family helped me also in making the decision to break away. My mother was in her nineties; she lived alone, had a heart condition, and needed my help caring for her, at least for a while. I took the first four months after leaving the university to be with her. Later, after my sister could take my place, I traveled to India to the Ashram of Osho and visit my new friend I had met in Bali.

CLUB MEDITATION AND MULTIVERSITY, POONA, INDIA—1995

I arrived in Bombay, India, also called Mumbai. My friend had arranged for a cab to drive me to Poona, a three-hour journey, to the Ashram. The roads were clogged with traffic—bikes, rickshas, trucks, and in the middle of it, an elephant pulling a heavy load. For a while, I watched with amazement. Then I watched with fear the way the driver maneuvered through this chaos, at times going off onto the banks to avoid an oncoming truck. I sat in the backseat covering my eyes in total surrender to what might happen. I finally had to laugh at the ridiculously dangerous situation. I made it safely to my friend's house.

The Ashram is a very beautiful environment. Creative and inspiring people come from all over the world seeking an alternative way of living, spiritual guidance through Osho's teachings and the meditations, taking place all day long in the beautiful white marble Buddha Hall, open to the surrounding gardens with white peacocks living in the rafters.

My days started early, just before daybreak. I would walk a few blocks to the Ashram wrapped in a scarf to keep me warm, passing small groups of people huddled around fires in the streets, beggars, small children on the sidewalk crying out for help, air filled with smoke.

I entered the gates of the Ashram to feel a sudden change in energy; all was peaceful and serene. At six in the morning, the Buddha Hall was filled with people, young and old, silent, all dressed in purple robes. We were starting the day with a dynamic meditation, shaking up the energy, shouting, moving our bodies, raising kundalini energy, then meditating, embracing stillness, then celebratory dancing. Breakfast in silence, followed by more mediation, whirling, dancing, kundalini meditations, listening to Osho's teachings, attending workshops, painting, self-hypnosis, self-awareness exercises. After evening Darshan, there was live music, jamming sessions of musicians spontaneously coming together to play as the rest of us danced to the music.

I took part in most of the meditations—kundalini, whirling, vipassana, all designed by Osho to break open resistance and still the mind. I had been resisting the unfamiliar ideas presented by Osho, was watching the disciples with suspicion and judgment. I could see a joy of living in them, a freedom of expression and a centeredness that I envied and wanted for myself. One night, I watched a ceremony happening inside the Buddha Hall from what I considered to be a safe distance. Outside, I felt "protected" in the shadow of palm trees. Suddenly, a tremendous rush of energy went through me like lightning, taking all my resistance away. I was free; it was an epiphany. I saw in a flash my unnecessary fears and boundaries. I saw two major emotions: love and fear. I realized that I do so much better with love, which melts the ice to a fluid state of being.

I came back to my home in New Mexico with trust and love. I was free to shape my days, to paint, to find a way to sustain myself with the work emotionally and physically. I was determined to make a livelihood with what I loved to do. I had set my intention; I could see it already coming my way by being in the moment without fear. I had a roof over my head, had food on the table, and had been given the gift of freedom to paint. "Yes!" I said.

After four months away, I looked at my work from a different perspective—without self judgement. A great inner shift in consciousness had taken place for me in Poona. My painting up to that point often showed the personal pain and anger I had experienced over the last few years, even going back to the war and my childhood. The joy of living, one of the messages in Osho's teachings, joy was missing in those paintings. Now I wanted to be conscious and grateful for the blessings, celebrate the moment, here and now. The process of painting can be healing, can bring in the light. It can help the artist let go of the darkness. Light is color; color is vibration that can transform.

I asked myself, *what do I have to say and share that is positive and contributes to the world?* The answer came to me by asking other questions: What is it I love? What brings me joy? Where does my eye wander? What does it rest on most often? What is the emotion I feel? What are the thoughts that follow? What wants to come to me to be noticed? That is where I need to go; that is what will support me.

CHAPTER 34

PAINTING IS MEDITATION

In meditation, we can transform the negative into the luminous, the positive, just as the oyster transforms the irritant into an iridescent pearl. The process of painting is a process of surrender to what wants to come in and be seen. I can reach for and bring in positive energy. I can bring in the light for myself and manifest it for others to experience in the painting. Yes, if positive energy is manifested in my work, will it not also support me financially and emotionally?

What subject matter might be most suited to this approach? What do I love in my life? I must paint what I love. I had long been inspired by nature. My MFA thesis was called "Hours in the Garden." The title referred to working the garden, providing meditation and clarity about the cycle of life—the beginning, the middle, and the end. Imagery of growth, organic beauty, and decay had been my theme for years. I saw the analogy between painting and gardening very clearly: Plant a seed with a choice of colors—light, uplifting, warm sunny palettes. Then have patience. See the seed emerge and grow. Nurture what shows itself in the garden and on the canvas.

While browsing in a used bookstore, I found a little book about Manet's last small paintings. He had painted bouquets of flowers brought to him by friends when he was bedridden. I studied his brushwork, his colors, the way the image of a flower emerged, the reflection of light on the water contained in the simple jar with rather abstract and gestural brushwork. I saw the way he used light and dark, value, contrast, and line. I tried to paint like Manet. Ha! Of course, I could not. But I discovered my own way of abstracting, allowing an image to come in without planning it or having a specific idea. I found that the imagery was unfolding in magical ways, emerging from memory deep in my consciousness. When pushing the paint around the canvas, I always had composition and color theory in my toolkit without thinking about it. My surrender to the process allowed what wanted to show itself. It required that I not force an idea or even a sketch onto that canvas. I had to start with color and feeling, to be open to see what would happen, surrender to the magic, go into the unknown. A form, a shape from a sketch, could come in later, making an area of color more specific; for example, drawing the outline of a leaf over a field of color would point to something more specific to contemplate. Drawing into color creates a tension between spaces or layers in a painting that I find exciting.

With the formal elements of painting: form, color composition—the "toolkit"—I had acquired in academic training, the painting was painting itself if I gave it space and time, gave myself to it, listened to what the painting was dreaming, what it needed. Then it could unfold in magical ways. The hard part was, and still is, letting the ego go out the door and listening to the still voice within, in dialogue with the voice coming from the painting.

The imagery often comes from experiences kept in memory, or should I say in the heart? In the process of painting, the memory becomes a living experience again, manifesting in form and color on the canvas. A painting has tangible energy that transmits itself to the viewer like electricity running through a live wire. The viewer can, if he or she is aware and open for it, feel the joy or sadness, the dark or the light energy the artist has experienced in the process of creating the image. A good example of this may be Picasso's *Guernica*, a large painting about the bombing of Guernica by the Nazis in support of Franco. The horror of the event and the artist's fury about it is clearly communicated; it is impossible not to feel that energy. An example of an opposite emotional message might be a painting by Matisse, The Dance, in which figures dance in a circle holding hands emitting a joyful presence and togetherness.

In my work which is abstract and often nonobjective, the energetic vehicles are color, form, and the dance of the brushwork, which may be fast moving or slow and gentle, and can, like a dance movement, transmit joyful energy.

When I came back from India in 1995, I had just enough money to sustain myself for three months, the time I gave myself to create a portfolio for presentation to local galleries in search of representation. Santa Fe in the '90s was a thriving art market. Many collectors came from all over the world. I did have work for sale in galleries in Denver, Boulder, and Houston. The work that sold mostly was my work on paper—the pastels, which by the time the gallery took 50 percent, provided me with a few hundred dollars each. To sustain me—to have enough money to pay my bills—I needed to create a portfolio of canvases that would sell at higher prices. A plan was needed.

A local Santa Fe gallery would make it easier for me to supply the work. There would be no travel or shipping costs involved, and there would be an opportunity for a closer working relationship with the gallery through studio visits and conversations with the staff members. I had not explored the local galleries during my time teaching. I had been lazy, relying on my monthly paycheck. Why bother? I had been asked to show my work by recommendations between gallery owners in Colorado and Texas without much of my own effort to reach out for representation. New Mexico was different; it was a new frontier. I was intimidated by the "second-largest art market in the country" and had resisted approaching the galleries. I got used to that safety blanket, but now I didn't have it anymore!

After three intense months working in the studio every day, I had several strong canvases to show. I walked Canyon Road—the "gallery road" in Santa Fe—up and down with a portfolio of my work. It was summer by now; my timing to fit into the tourist season was off. I received one rejection after another. "Come back at the end of the year," one gallery owner said. "Wrong time," said another. "We have already scheduled all artists for the season." I walked by one gallery I had not been in before. Curious, I went in and liked what I saw: the work of Hal Larsen, an abstract artist. His paintings were large, in strong colors, rather masculine.

The young saleswoman was German, and even more astonishing, she was a member of the same Ashram in India I had just come back from. This was another serendipitous connection like several others I had experienced before in my life! She told me the owner wanted to show another artist, she liked my work, and would talk to the owner.

Within days, I was showing my new paintings there, and I was happy! The owner's wife, a gallery owner herself, suggested right away that I should double my prices. I started to sell there consistently. I felt once again that guidance and the power of intention had come through in mysterious ways. Celebration! I was grateful! I showed there for several years and gained confidence; I could make a livelihood from my work.

CHAPTER 35

THE BUSINESS OF ART

There was a rock in the path—the gallery owner was difficult to work with. Art is taken in on a commission basis, bringing in good money for the owner without investment in an inventory. The owner willingly gave huge discounts to close a sale. It often felt like a betrayal to me and to the integrity of the work. I decided to find another place to sell my work.

Once again, I walked Canyon Road without any specific focus. I came into a little artist-run studio showing realistic popular "postcard images" that tourists to Santa Fe would buy. The artist/owner told me that she sold her work well; in fact, she could not keep up with the demand. While she worked in the studio-gallery, she was constantly "distracted" by walk-in visitors keeping her from painting.

I volunteered to help her by working the sales in the gallery, with the condition that I could show my work with her also. She agreed to give me one wall in the gallery to show my paintings. Because I had experience in gallery work from my apprenticeship in Germany, I was excited to be out in the marketplace again.

After a few months, I proved that I could sell her work as well as my own. She decided to let me have the entire gallery space for myself. Her son was ill, and she needed time away from the business. I took the chance, not thinking twice about the risk of the financial commitment. I had just sold a painting and could put a payment down for the rent. I was now able to create independence for myself: I had my own gallery on Canyon Road. People in the business gave me well-intentioned advice: "you must have a business plan plus one year's expenses in the bank." I did not have either. Once again, I relied on my own way of doing things. I took a leap of faith to live frugally and by surprise.

My early training in the gallery in Germany came through for me. I knew how to set up a welcoming space and quickly learned how to close a sale and create a personal connection to the buyer. I was doing well. My work sold. People loved meeting the artist and hearing my thoughts about each piece. I could make a connection to buyers and see for myself where the work was going. Getting to know my audience and hear the responses to my work, gave me a real sense of what my "mission" was: to bring light and positive energy into people's living rooms.

One day, I had a great conversation about my ideas and background with one collector. He bought three of my paintings, and as he walked out of the gallery, he turned around and said, "Let me know if you ever need help." Years later, after he bought several more paintings from me, he donated a large piece to the permanent collection of the Albuquerque Museum of Art.

Another day, a couple came in and right away asked me if I was German. Then they told me to go back to where I had come from. Shocked at first, I realized there must be Holocaust history in their family. I do not know how I managed to have a conversation about art and probably more personal things, but when they left, they invited me to visit them at their home in Kansas, should I ever pass through their area. At times words came to me that were exactly what needed to be said. At other times, a person would see my work and come back years later to buy. After many years, these experiences still fill me with wonder.

I invented a system for bookkeeping in handwritten ledgers. Numbers and spreadsheets had not been my strongest points for sure. Slowly, with determination, I learned to use a computer. For a while, I did not even have email, which would be unthinkable today. An artist friend from graduate school whose work I also showed, helped me with computer skills, standing behind me, telling me what keys to push. Thanks, my friend!

I wanted to show the work of other artists along with my own to make the studio-gallery more appealing to a wider audience. Even though the space was small, I decided on two painters, friends whose work I loved, and one printmaker. I did well for all of us. I soon needed help; I could not be there all the time and have time in the studio. I tried painting in the gallery, but people walking in looking over my shoulder disrupted my meditative way of painting. Every time I had to put down the brush to help a visitor, I lost the dialogue with the painting. With part-time help, I was able to work at home three days a week, but I still carried the heavy load of a business owner: decision making and financial commitment in the very seasonal, high-rent market of Santa Fe, with almost half of the year being very slow in tourism and, therefore, buyers. Between 2000 and 2004 online internet business was not a reality yet; we relied on walk-in business. The proceeds from the good months had to be enough to cover expenses through the slow months.

The logistics of running a business wore me down. A full-time director would have enabled me to be less involved energetically, but that was not quite possible financially. Maybe I also was not willing to surrender control of my gallery to someone else. I did not like any object or painting to be moved around in the gallery; I had to have it "my way," which was not much fun for anyone working for me. I wanted staff members to be focused on communicating the message of the work through an intelligent informed conversation without being pushy. I wanted their interactions to be courteous and personal in a meaningful way. I did not know how to manage from a distance or be gentle in my guidance. I was not savvy enough as a manager. Some choices I regret in hindsight—should have—could have.

After four years, I felt a need for that solitary life again. I had to ask myself, *where is my focus? Am I a gallery person or am I a painter?* Maybe I approached the question too exclusively for one or the other. After four years, with 9/11 in the middle of it, I felt my energy and spiritual well-being drowning in the daily "stuff" of running a gallery. In addition to the time in the gallery came the two-hour roundtrip commute to the gallery, cutting my quiet time short. I decided to close my retail operation and find representation with another gallery again and take some time out to focus on just doing the work.

The next years gave me time to myself, but again, I had to move my work from gallery to gallery several times. The personal connection to the client was missing. My work was shown alongside other artists' work, often not a good mixture of voices. It is an art form to hang a show, and I was often critical of what I saw done. Often the staff had a difficult time selling abstraction. They wanted trees—more conventional work.

A good, successful dealer has a vision for the artist's work, believe in it, accept and encourage changes in the work overtime. A good dealer is an entire support system for the artist and the collector. He or she can curate a collector's selection of work, build a relationship of trust, based on his or her understanding and "eye" for art. Representation in a walk-in, bricks-and-mortar gallery is often the first connection to an artist's work. It is more powerful to see a painting in person; there is that energy directly shining at you. I loved to do it all, but to create the work is the priority. Time and energy are limited as I found out after trying several times to run my own gallery.

CHAPTER 37

THE POWER OF PAINT AND COLOR

Art washes away from the soul the dust of everyday life

(Picasso is assumed to have said this). The magic of art, light and color is what can give me that jolt in my stomach when I look at some original work that goes beyond the postcard image. I am not satisfied with an image that offers instant recognition, maybe brings up a memory, but asks no question.

Taught to make sense of something with a conceptual approach, we instinctively look for something to recognize—a story, a horse, a face—even in nonobjective abstract art. Once we see that "rabbit", a narrative is suggested that cannot be reversed. The horse, the fish, the rabbit or face, becomes a story, it is what we will see and maybe that is alright too. Another approach is to see the "paint"—the texture, the brushwork, the color and composition—and then listen to the emotional responses we have to the vibration of light and color. Light is color and is alchemy. The lack of recognizable imagery in nonobjective art makes it easier to notice our feelings, good or maybe not so good as they may be. Why do I feel this way? This is an important question to ask when looking at art. A painting can pierce the veil to a different reality. A painting can change every day, one can see something different or is asked something new. For me, to connect with a painting, it must feed my soul, it must ask a question, not give an answer or illustrate what we already know.

Over the years, I have been fortunate; I have been able to experience the magic of art in people's responses. I have seen visitors transfixed, even weep in front of a painting. Something mysterious happens. It is the power of art speaking to our spiritual bodies more than the intellectual. The beauty and grace of art, representational or nonobjective, both speak to our humanity and the human condition. This is how art can touch the soul.

It is thought that prehistoric man painted images of animals important to them, maybe even considered to be sacred. The artists painted images of horses, bison, lions, deer and others on cave walls using torches to illuminate the space while they worked. Most of the animals depicted were not the animals they hunted for food, and they represented more than a story. We see layers of sometimes overlapping images done over time. The painters used very primitive tools and pigments from the earth. Bears most likely lived in the caves they decorated. The people lived outside of the caves in the open, and to enter the caves was dangerous. Maybe the caves were spaces for rituals to honor the animals. In some caves bear skulls were placed in a special way to suggest a shrine. Maybe the process of painting was the ritual?

In the prehistoric Lascaux cave paintings, created about 20,000 years ago, we find only one human figure represented in the midst of all the animal images. The figure is thought to possibly be a shaman. He is lying down and has an erection. He is either in a trance or dying, wearing a bird mask. He has a bird-topped staff and is positioned next to an injured bull who confronts the man; both are possibly between life and death. These powerful and mysterious images ask questions of us and make us wonder about their meaning. What was the motivation for these images? What do they say to us today? No matter what "the story" may be, these images have a power to touch us today. The prehistoric artists were highly accomplished and much more connected to nature than we are today, even with all our knowledge we have acquired over thousands of years. They created something outside of themselves to touch something larger than themselves. To create something outside of myself is also my path.

Lascaux Cave Painting

photo

JOURNAL ENTRY JUNE 8TH

EPIPHANY

I moved a mountain this morning, working on a painting, carefully, afraid I would not do the right thing. Afraid to do something coming from my heart that is different from what I had done in the past, something my eyes have seen for long outside my window but have not dared to put onto canvas. What I see is so beautiful, and where do I go from there?

I can say that "we" have done it today in what seemed like a very short time. I am inside and out. I am one with the Universe. This moment has no question unanswered, no problem unsolved. This is all there is—this one moment. I am drunk with the power of life. This moment everything comes together so beautifully and so perfectly. When I surrender, I can move a mountain. I am *that*.

I will look at the painting again tomorrow morning when I am sober from the wine of joy and celebration. My pond is full of fish again. The peonies are in ecstasy, a crescendo of life.

CHAPTER 38

THE PROCESS OF PAINTING

I believe color, without an image, like music or words, creates vibrations that lead to emotions. I am drawn to harmony. This is true for music, poetry, and painting. Disharmony—the arrangement of forms and color in a jarring way—can work if there is a "resolution" worked into the composition.

I want resolution; I want harmony in composition and color. Composition is the arrangement of forms in the pictorial area. Art in the Western world since the Renaissance often relies on the triangle for resolution. For example, the Madonna holding the baby Jesus with angels or other figures forming a triangle result in a steady, balanced "harmonious" composition. This same idea can also be used in abstraction by using color in the same way; for example, by placing three yellow shapes in a triangular relationship within the pictorial area.

Color can make us feel any range of emotions. Many theories about how color affects our emotions have been developed by artists and scientists. A sunflower can make us happy, and the color blue can be interpreted as soothing or even sad (I am feeling blue). Red is a very "active" color, coming forward calling for attention. A warm red can cause a positive association or warm feeling. To the contrary, a dark red that has some blue mixed in giving it a purplish hue gives not such a warm feeling at all. Besides a personal emotional response to color coming from our own experiences, color and its symbolism can also be defined by culture and association. The color red or blue have been politicized in certain cultures, for example the colors in national flags might give a clue to symbolism and association.

I believe that the energy of a painting is in the vibrations of light or color. Light is color, a prism breaks light up into a rainbow color. Each color has different frequencies we respond to. The response to the vibration of color is energetic and automatic and is usually unconscious. If I try to invite a certain response, I must be aware of my color choices. I say "try" because a viewer's response depends on his or her background and personality, both of which are outside of my influence. My personal practice is to use mostly a warm palette with some contrasting cool and dark colors and forms. Quantity and quality of colors are important to consider for harmony. Just as in baking or cooking, how much and how saturated, is important for any recipe to be successful.

Much has been written about color theory. Wassily Kandinsky is often called the father of abstraction. His ideas on the subject have been very influential in my work. In his book, *Concerning the Spiritual in*

BRIGITTE BRÜGGEMANN | 115

Art, first published in 1910, Kandinsky wrote, "Color directly influences the soul. Color is the keyboard, the eyes are the hammers, the soul is the piano with many strings. The artist is the hand that plays, touching one key or another purposively, to cause vibrations in the soul.

Kandinsky also wrote about the "inner necessity" in *Concerning the Spiritual in Art*:

> The artist must have something to say, for mastery over form is not his goal but rather adapting of a form to its inner meaning. This does not mean that the artist is to instill forcibly into his work some deliberate meaning. As has been said: the creation of a work of art is a mystery. So long as artistry exists there is no need for theory or logic to direct the painter's action. The inner voice of the soul tells what form s/he needs, whether inside or outside nature. Every artist knows, who works with feeling, how suddenly the right form flashes upon him.

What is created by many artists today is often conceptual. This of course is an equally valid approach to making art. For me, the process of painting must remain a mystery, and it is my choice to allow for the unknown to come in. And it should be so. When I say, "I do not know what I am doing," I do not mean I don't have the skills. It merely means that I surrender to what wants to come into the work through me. Call it anything you want—muse, inspiration, magic, creation. It remains a mystery, and that is the true wonder of it all: to go into the unknown with every painting.

Sometimes I need to steer away from what feels "precious." There are moments in making a painting when I feel great about a passage—one part in the painting, maybe a brushstroke, a combination of colors, textures, or even an image that tells a "story." When a passage does not connect with the rest of the painting, the painting is not resolved. I work around the precious part, try to make everything else work as one, and often end up having to paint out the precious part—paint out the story that may be a distraction taking the painting into a place it does not want to be; it does not work, the dialogue between the painting and my inner voice stops. The attachment to one part can stop my creative energy from flowing in the work. I recognize that feeling; I am stuck or trapped by attachment.

I want to find what I do not know yet—or have forgotten. I may have had an experience that comes back during the process of painting and comes alive in the painting—manifests itself, wants to be shown, not necessarily as a story, recognizable image, or narrative. The gesture of one brush mark can speak about a branch moving in the wind or water reflecting light.

There are times when a painting just happens. I feel as if no time has passed in the process. I get lost in the meditative state of painting; everything works. That is the magic that keeps me going through the hard times, keeps me with a painting when it is real "work," when it is difficult, a struggle, when I lose confidence, when I want to give up, thinking I will never do another painting. I have days like that, then I must remember the blessing when the light comes through; I yearn for it to happen again. If I do not go into the studio and pick up the brush, it will never happen. Fear of failure does not do anything at all. I must remember the gift I have been given and celebrate it with gratitude and prayer while holding the brush in my hand.

JOURNAL ENTRY

Sunday morning, three pretty horses by the fence.

Painted pony white and brown

swishing long tails.

Dogs barking at their feet.

What am I here for?

I had an idea last night—

drawings of flowers,

pretty things. Why?

Beauty and grace

dance with the light.

Is that my necessary fire?

GATEWAY

What a beautiful day today. Suddenly it is summer. I want to be in the garden watching the fish in the pond, watching flowers grow and birds fly about. I have a painting going, a large drawing coming together with many brush marks, lines, high-frequency colors making my heart sing, coming together like a tapestry, a weaving of lines filled with light. I am watching. I opened the angelic gateway to the heart, have let fall away distractions and activities. The silence I have immersed myself into, this place filled with light and love, brings forth another luminous painting.

Dancing with the Light

oil

Quiet morning, I sit in the sun

with Blackfoot purring.

He loves the warmth of the sun

and my touch.

I easily slip into a space of silence and peace,

a space of no thought early in the morning,

a precious place to be.

Light streams through the prism in the window

casting rainbow wheels on the walls.

I travel on these wheels

attached to my soul like roller skates,

joyfully celebrating my existence.

The old lady next door is watching me,

smiling, she remembers.

PARADOX

I woke up to a cloudy sky, my soul is clouded also.

Did I have a dream I do not remember?

Are my hopes and desires clouding my vision?

I cannot see the horizon.

I speak to myself:

the blue sky is always there,

who is with you all the time,

behind you, beside you, and above you?

I feel left alone.

I created this space around me.

Nobody comes through, or climbs over the wall around my garden,

the wall around my heart?

I am reaching out. Silence is answering:

Be still. Do you not see the small gestures that come to you all the time?

A friend giving you a small chocolate, a note, a look, a hug.

Oh, I forgot those gestures.

Clouds bring on the rain and my tears.

Remember: clouds weep, garden sprouts.

Yesterday I talked with a friend about these dark clouds hanging over us at times. We can't see any reason to bring on this dark mood; it is just there. We decided that it may be energy passing through us coming from who knows where, passing through a receptive and sensitive soul absorbing that energy like a sponge. Maybe it is our task to clear out that darkness and transform it into light—maybe. I must clear the darkness within my own heart. How often do I fail? I cannot see anymore. I must go into the studio and paint so I can see again. There I am alone but not lonely.

The House of the Beaver

pastel

BRIGITTE BRÜGGEMANN | 121

JOURNEY

So lass uns Abschied nehmen wie zwei Sterne

durch jenes Übermass von Nacht getrennt,

das eine Nähe ist, die sich an Ferne erprobt

und an dem Fernsten sich erkennt.

—Rainer Maria Rilke

From *The Selected Poetry of Rainer Maria Rilke*

My translation:

Then, let us say farewell

Like two stars

Separated by vastness of the night

that is also closeness

experiencing itself through distance

recognizing itself by the farthest point.

A dove

sitting on a wire

sweetly calling its mate.

Apricot tree

blossoms opened in the night.

Bach

music flowing like the river.

Coming back from a long journey.

I am experiencing the open space,

the vastness of the night,

a new sense of wonder.

The eternal mirrored in starry nights,

my heart opens, my soul streams toward the endless.

My house has become an extension of my self; even more, it is a manifestation of self. I am surrounded with things of beauty, things I love from the past and present. With love and care, I created a garden in this arid high desert environment. I find my nature in nature. Wildlife comes to visit. Birds come to stay. The little fox cruises by the chicken house, looking over his shoulder back at me, smiling. The roadrunner with a snake in his beak knocks on my window to bring me an offering. The first hummingbird comes to my kitchen window in the morning for a greeting. This is one-ness made real for me.

Summertime

photo of Brigitte's garden

It has been said: "Attachment" is not a good thing; we need to be ready to "die" metaphorically speaking. While I am here on this earth, in this body, I surround myself with beauty, create and walk in beauty, without apology. I am very connected to this place, and even though many times I wonder about the practicality of living forty minutes away from the city, the hospital, a grocery store, any event of interest can become difficult to reach eventually with aging. When the time comes, I will move—unless I am not. In the meantime, I enjoy my time by the river, especially in the summer when the living is easy.

PART 4
OTHER PLACES AND THINGS

Throughout my life, I have had a strong interest to see new places and other cultures. I am curious about the unfamiliar. I love this place here in New Mexico by the river, but I must fly away sometimes to find new images, new places, meet new people. I come back recharged and filled with appreciation for what has been given to me. My travels have taken me to many places: India, Bali, Thailand, Africa, many locations in Europe—Italy, France, Spain, Greece. I visit museums, see art, walk the streets, enjoy the food and the people. I spend several weeks, even months in one place, exploring the surrounding area at a leisurely pace with days at home (away from home) reading and painting.

In a few hours, I can be transplanted into a different reality. When I am away, I often wonder *does my place there in New Mexico exist?* This moment in time is all there is. I travel with my watercolors—a selection of colors that work for me—brushes and paper, a sketchbook, all in a small pack. Having a camera is important also, but before I set out each day, I choose to take either the sketchbook or the camera with me that day. I cannot switch back and forth without confusion. Seeing through the camera lens is different from seeing what I am sketching. So, I eliminate one or the other for the day. Sometimes I sketch from a train, bus, or car (if I am the passenger). Since things are passing by too fast for me to be able to focus on one thing, I draw very quickly whatever wants to be noticed. The arrangement of the forms on the paper is purely unconscious and driven by the moment. It is amazing and empowering that it usually works well to give an impression of the landscape.

When I get home after a day's excursion, I sit down and paint the same way, putting things together in a collage of images. This allows for the emotional experience, the spirit of a place, to come through, which is more meaningful for me than creating a postcard picture illustration of the day.

Andalusia

watercolor

MY JOURNEY TO THE EAST
VENICE—FOG,

A scale of shadowy grays, light fragmented by fog, breaking into thousand diamonds. Boats on the canals. Walking, walking. I walk up across bridges into the fog and down again into the narrow streets, so narrow that, if I touch the wall on one side of the street with one hand, at the same time I can touch the wall on the other side. History, facades telling stories—Venetian red, mustard yellow, and flake white, colors reminiscent of the fine silken Venetian fabrics in elegant designs. Water everywhere, above and below. Mystery in time and place, my consciousness is shifting.

Fishes in the canals. Angels on rooftop spires looking down,

blessing those below who see them.

Doves fly between domes and turrets.

The shrill cries of seagulls,

splashing of boats in the water,

the clicking of my heels on the cobblestones,

sounds I hear.

I stop at the fish market, pull out my sketchbook, and draw the beautiful lines and shapes of the fishes on the tables. Church bells ringing. Laughter. The vendors smile at me in disbelief.

Campo Della Pescaria

watercolor

Bali

Morning in Ubud

After a long exhausting flight, I woke up from the sounds of the night: bird calls, doves, a throbbing grand orchestra, the sounds of life—primal, real. I have arrived in body and spirit. My mind is still in yesterday. Body moving too fast for what mind can handle.

I sit down outdoors for a heavenly breakfast: banana pancakes, fruit, strong Balinese coffee served by a beautiful smiling young woman wrapped in a colorful sarong and a hibiscus flower in her hair. Every wall surface is covered with texture, carved ornaments, man-made or natural. Walls are covered with moss and vines. The moist air smells fragrant and delicious like the food. I see little shrines everywhere—witnesses, traces of ceremony important in this culture, honoring the forces of nature and the pantheon of Hindu gods. People are friendly, sending me beautiful smiles, genuine and open. The beauty takes my breath away. Love for life finds a door, carved and gilded, into my heart and soul. The mind is not far behind now.

Evening, full moon. I hopped on a scooter taxi tonight to go to a fire dance in one of the main temples in town. The story acted out in dance comes from a Hindu legend: a love story, damsel in distress, the fight of good against evil ending with victory of love over darkness. The movements of the young girl dancers are beautiful, very slow with exaggerated hand movements. The fire dance was at the end of the performance. The male dancer, in a trance, walked over red-hot cinders, kicking them into the audience. I sat in the first row and had to pull my feet up high to avoid the burning coals—I was not in a trance, but the music and chanting made me sleepy. After the performance, my scooter taxi was not waiting for me as I had arranged before to take me home, so I walked, under a full moon above, music coming out of bars and restaurants. I am singing along, with my heart open.

Sunday

A cloudy day after a lovely rain in the night. A cough has slowed me down, and maybe that is good body wisdom.

I saw some traditional Balinese paintings today at the Arma House . Many of the stories from Hindu legends are told in these paintings, again, the stories about good and evil. A conversation with my neighbor here at the bungalows is going that way as well: he believes the world is taken over by evil forces, conspiracies, and corruption in politics. I have noticed that people on the path can go into this space of Armageddon. I am putting my head in the sand; I do not want to live in fear.

Today I visited a quiet very beautiful temple. As in most temples, in the center of the courtyard stands a large plumeria tree. The white fragrant flowers represent birth and love, spring and new beginnings, these are the flower I wore in my hair on my wedding day. In the large trunk of the tree was a hollow space large enough to hold an egg-shaped large smooth rock—a shrine in a tree.

I felt good energy and stayed for a while before hiking up the trail along a ridge between two steep river valleys, gurgling water rushed through a jungle of vegetation, rice paddies terraced to follow the terrain, I felt the breeze in my hair. At each rice paddy if found a little shrine with offerings made from palm leaves woven into artful little things and adorned with small flowers.

Just when I got too hot, a little roadside cafe appeared. I sat down on the patio overlooking the rice fields. Sitting among pillows covered in beautiful fabrics, I cooled off with a Mango Lassie, watching women wearing big straw hats, harvest the rice while ducks roamed the fields. The peak of Mount Agung, the sacred mother mountain, towering in the background, clouded in a halo of mist.

Candidasa

Evening, I listened to the waves of the Indian Ocean, watched the lights of fishing boats going out into the night. A large ship anchored in a distance was illuminated with strings of lights. The nocturnal dark-green and black water moving endlessly, waves crashing under the terrace of the open-air dining room. The surge was strong; I felt a pull into a strange unfamiliar place. Waking at two in the morning, I heard birds outside, the nightly twitter concert. I felt a shift in consciousness; I was about to leave to the shores of another reality.

Silent world

Early in the morning, a boat takes me out to a lagoon. I float, snorkeling in the Indian Ocean. Schools of fish surround me, moving like a flock of birds turning in synchronicity, taking me with them, swimming jewels, looking at me, coming close almost touch me, then turning with a flip of the tail. Opalesque, shimmering greens, yellows, blue Jewel tones, incredible shapes, striped, dotted and square, corals in amazing shapes. This is creation at its most flamboyant and imaginative! I am totally in the moment, part of a silent world at peace. Coming up for air, I see the boat that had brought me here sitting on the waves like a giant yellow spider

Different Realities

    pastel

Sidemen

My place for another week is in Sidemen, a village high in the mountain. Rain is coming down, thunder. Outside my window, Mt. Agung is veiled in clouds. Maybe tomorrow I will see her, the mother mountain I came here for. My room is lovely, high pyramid ceiling, windows all around surrounded by a large terrace with a view of the tropical landscape with the towering mountain in the background. It is quiet here except for occasional tourist chatter from the bar restaurant below, some motorcycles, and a chain saw nearby; the noise stops with the rain. I am curious how I will adjust to this sitting-still-time. I wanted this for myself: more meditation, pray for the painting to come to me

At dinner I was surrounded by couples, groups, and families. I am the only single woman. Self-conscious, I fled back to my room, to my fortress. I sit now in my queen-size bed with the mosquito netting all around me. It feels like the bed of my childhood, the boat I imagined it to be—safe.

I am listening to the Beatles:

"All things must pass"[4]

I hold on to my lovely adventure.

"It is not always gonna be that gray"[5]

Doubt is not far away: What am I doing here, a woman by herself? What's wrong with me? Everybody here has a friend or two to travel with; am I questioning my life? No, honey, don't. I am ready to bed down with my dreams. The CD plays:

"You may say I am a dreamer, but I am not the only one ..."[6]

Late afternoon

I have been still as the water in the pond where the lotus grows. Am I starting to grow lovely algae on my skin? I took a nap in the afternoon, went for a swim with the hope the sun would come out. Then more sitting, just sitting, looking out with nothing in particular on my mind, watching the shifting light in the landscape, dark clouds moving around the Mother Mountain. I paint a little, very slowly, giving myself permission to have no objective. That is good for me now. It has been a struggle to come to that.

No mind. Even writing seems a stretch.

Nothing is important. How lucky can I get?

I am still trying to paint. Stop trying. Meditation instead.

---

[4] "All Things Must Pass"—lyrics by George Harrison.
[5] "All Things Must Pass"—lyrics by George Harrison.
[6] "Imagine"—lyrics by John Lennon.

Surrender, the magic word. It sounds so easy but is so hard to do. I throw my whole body against whatever it is that gets in the way. Looking at this abundance of shapes—green, green, green—brings out a timidity in my efforts to paint.

People tell me that it is not important—to paint or not to paint. Sorry, I can't agree, even though I might want to. I know in my heart that my well-being depends on the process of translating what I feel about what I see—into images.

This afternoon I did pretend painting is not important. I took up the brush without much enthusiasm, like picking up a spoon in the kitchen, and there, it happened. Something broke me away from painting timidly and tightly. This is different: I loaded up the brush with brilliant color and went for it. One painting after another came to me. I got some good ones! Happy? You bet. The gods do like to test me at times: Do you want this? Yes, I say.

A day of ceremony.

I followed the sound of the gamelans and the decorations—yellow-golden umbrellas and beautiful ornaments woven with palm leaves. At the entrance of the village, steep steps led up to the temple. Young boys and men sat up at the gate, dressed in the local costume, mostly white sarongs, and tight headscarves.

I asked them if it was okay for me to enter. In respect of the local custom, I had dressed in a sarong and wore a scarf around my shoulders. With big smiles, they waved and urged me to come on up, joking and laughing at me catching my breath as I climbed up the steep steps. Inside the temple, women and children sat together in their finery. Offerings of flowers and fruit were piled up in front of an ornate carved and painted shrine. The men were busy tending a fire. Everybody was very friendly, and I felt welcome. A young man came up to me and, in very good English, explained what was going on: The symbols of the gods held in the temple, will be put into a shrine for the ceremony and transported to another location. "We cannot talk about what the symbols are," he told me. "The deep meaning of the ritual is secret." A lengthy ceremony started with prayers, a priest performing the rites. The shrine was lifted onto the shoulders of men and carried out of the temple in a procession announced to the villagers lined up along the route with gamelan gongs, cymbals, and drums. The procession wound through the village and up the mountain to another temple in the forest, where the symbols were blessed with water from a holy spring. I left the ceremony to walk back to the hotel. I am grateful for this experience and the friendly and welcoming smiles to me, a curious stranger.

Sitting. Looking. Listening, the rain is coming down. Animal noises stop. I am watching the restlessness in myself dissolve with the rain. There is nowhere to go really. I could easily do the sightseeing thing again, but this is what I came here for: to soak up the energy of this exotic place and paint. I have some ginger and lemon tea with honey to soothe my cough that is still with me.

The young girl at the front desk is so animated and open. She is looking after the little kitten that was run over by the taxi at my arrival. I witnessed the accident; the kitten was hit by a cab backing out of the driveway. I was horrified to see the kitten hurt, I thought it was a bad omen and kept thinking about it, rewinding the movie in my mind's eye. It keeps me here somehow; I want to see the kitten walk again. Kitty seems to improve, sleeping a lot, curled up in a little box covered with a shawl to match the fur colors of brown and black. The girl shared some of her life in this small mountain village she grew up in. I sensed that there was a longing in her for a larger world.

Cat and Goose

watercolor

Firefly—fly

Evening has come I am listening to "While My Guitar Gently Weeps."[7] A firefly is floating by.

In the morning, I took a long walk through the rice paddies and came upon a hanging bridge swinging over a rushing creek. At first, I hesitated. Should I just turn and go back? No. I took courage. Holding on to the ropes on each side, I negotiated the slats. Wide-open spaces between them revealed the torrent below.

Titra Ganga

I hired a driver to take me to a sacred spring at the water temple. We drove through rice fields with amazing vistas of Mount Agung. My guide told me that this area was devastated by a volcanic eruption in the 1960s. The village was destroyed. Many people chose not to leave in time and perished.

Bemo Story

watercolor

---

[7] "While My Guitar Gently Weeps"—lyrics by George Harrison.

Today the fields are flooded with water, and new bright green growth is emerging. The pattern of the terraces follows the shape of the slope. The volcano is circled by clouds.

The water temple is very beautiful. Tall lotus flowers in the large ponds reach straight up about two feet from the water's surface. The stems are surrounded by huge round lotus leaves floating on the surface. Puddles and drops of water on the leaves reflect the blue sky and clouds. The many ponds give this temple an expansive energy; I experience joy.

Coming back to the village, a cremation was happening. In Hindu tradition, the dead are burned in the open at a special site for just that purpose. A very simple coffin—a crude wooden box—sat on a dirt mound, covered with offerings and flowers brought up by locals. It looked as if the people surrounding the coffin were telling each other stories about the departed, there was laughter and chatter. No tears: according to Hindu tradition, one does not cry in public. This went on until the platform was set on fire, quickly engulfing the coffin in flames. Everybody left. I found this strange, recalling my own experience at my mother's cremation when I cried my eyes out. It made me sad seeing the flames. Some things are universal: last offerings of flowers to go with the body.

I am on the way home, going West.

Hometown: Stuttgart, Market Day.

A must: I visit the flower market; lively and lovely. Many stands with umbrellas are grouped around the statue of Friedrich Schiller, the beloved native son. With the poet's laurel wreath on his head, he looks down benevolently onto the scene. Oh, I enjoy being around people. Maybe solitude is not right for me anymore? It is both I want at times. I lit a candle for Mutti in the Stiftskirche and said a prayer.

Stuttgart

watercolor

Hazy spring day at my friend's house.

A light haze floated over the city promising a warm day. Springtime! Everything is coming to life, eager to grow and reach for the sun: lilac, wisteria, peonies, and all the lovely spring flowers. Meadows are filled with wildflowers between apple trees, clouds of white blossoms with a little bit of pink. Pear trees stand proud, shaped like their fruit.

I have slowed down, enjoy sitting, reading, talking, cooking with my friend. My time in Stuttgart, the conversations, surrounded by friends I grew up with is a lovely, precious time. I am feeling good but am already longing for change, heading for the open road again.

Tomorrow morning "Reise nach Italien."

Many European artists traveled to Italy in search of inspiration during the eighteenth century or even earlier. It was a dangerous journey that took weeks, not the few hours it takes today. Travelers had to cross the Alps on foot, horseback or wagons facing many roadside dangers.

In his book, Italian *Journey: 1786–1788*, Johann Wolfgang von Goethe wrote, "Nothing can be compared to the new life that the discovery of another country provides for a thoughtful person. Although I am still the same, I believe to have changed to the bones."

Following in the steps of many artists before me today, Italy here I come, seeking a pilgrimage, another shift, another city, less familiar. There is much art to explore. Once again, I am putting myself on the edge of my seat: to be a stranger in a foreign country.

Florence

My apartment is just around the corner from the Piazza della Signoria where a copy of Michelangelo's David and other famous sculptures attract crowds of tourists. A few steps away are the Uffizi Galleries. I go to see the many Italian Renaissance paintings. One of my favorites is the timeless *Primavera* by Botticelli. I visit my favorite portraits of the Medici. Leaving the Galleries, I pass many vendors selling copies of those famous paintings. I have heard often that Renaissance art is dead; this makes me sad for the lack of understanding of the timeless beauty of these images. When I wander the streets, I find countless graffiti paintings on the walls of Florence using these Renaissance images with a contemporary twist. Now I am happy to see that Renaissance art is alive and well with the people of Florence.

Graffiti based on Botticelli's 1495 Portrait of Dante, photo

I went out "shopping" with no intention for anything, just trying on a different look. I found a shop selling leather gloves, offering a rainbow of different colors, selling only gloves, imagine that; this is Italy. Passing by the Piazza Della Republica, I listened to a three-man Rumanian band: violin, cello, guitar. They played so well! This is entertainment without a ticket, donations welcome. The three musicians were trained during the communist era at the conservatory of music in Romania, well known in their own country. With the iron curtain falling and the political changes, they were out of work and opportunities. They managed to come to the West. Now they play in the streets of Florence. All three live in one room taking in on average about two hundred euros a day among them. I enjoyed the music—easy listening, well-known songs, gypsy music, toe-tapping kind of music. I wondered how they feel about living in exile.

Art makes me feel good; it takes the dust of the soul. This morning I woke up feeling great. How wonderful to be here. I am grateful. No more feeling self-conscious being the senior among the young students in my Italian class or being alone in the midst of masses of people, groups, couples, families, and friends, roaming the streets of Florence. I am happy today, but just yesterday along with the rain, came a bit of an emotional cloud: I felt homesick. What exactly does that mean? Longing for some familiarity a human connection beyond *buon giorno and come stai?* Wishing for a conversation or maybe just being surrounded by something or someone touching me more deeply. I bought some pears at the greengrocer. I asked for them in Italian. The kind man smiled and corrected me in a way that touched me. It is the little things that make a difference.

It rained very hard—so hard it came through the window. The ancient window in this Renaissance building does not close very tightly over the sofa. Oops, quick, get some pots to catch the water. This too did pass—the rain and the emotional cloud.

May 5

My mother's and my daughter's birthdays are today, a blessed day. I found a plaque on a house across the Ponte Vecchio, the poet's corner, honoring a poet who has lived here.

In this rippling of light,

the Arno River right there,

golden light rippling on the water.

People have lived here and gone,

other's taking their place,

taking all things serious

filling every day with importance

only to disappear into nothingness,

maybe, if lucky, a plaque somewhere, or forgotten.

A year later, a painting came to me. This brief experience became the source for something that will last: a painting in someone's living room in Atlanta, Georgia.

In This Rippling of Light

oil

GIARDINO BANDINI

I woke up tired this morning, tired of the stone walls and the lack of sun inside my apartment. So, the little bird at my soul's window said, "Go to the Giardino Bandini. It is close—across the bridge a few steps." I could smell flowers through the walls.

This is a truly Italian garden—formal terraces, steps, and niches, gods and goddesses, stone lions and other cats guarding the place, vistas I could not imagine. Between azaleas, camellias, irises, and roses I see the Duomo, church bells ringing—for the love of God, Firenze at my feet. I return to my apartment content, tired with a different sort of fatigue in my feet.

May 10

Giorgio Morandi, *"Pittore di luce e di silenzio."*

Painter of light and silence. How does one paint silence?

Morandi knew.

How does one paint light?

Morandi did.

In a gallery, I saw an incredible collection of Morandi paintings. Bliss! So many of his oils in one place! Subtle shifts of light and shapes. I had never seen his florals before or any of his landscapes. Here it all was, side by side along with many of his famous still lifes—bottles with shadows or without. The bottles' forms take on a human quality—the way they sit in space facing each other or turning away, slim or fat, like people. Three paintings of his house in Bologna have a sensibility that speaks about "home" that I understand. It is interesting how he plays with details, adding or eliminating. The light in these paintings moves my heart and feeds my soul.

Then, I stumbled upon a Gelateria across the street. I see the colors of Morandi's palette matching the hues of the gelato. Pleasure! In Italia, they certainly know how to make gelato and art—tasty, such taste, such joy! Two young Japanese girls were so delighted with their generous three scoops of gelato piled up high on a cone, they took a selfie before they licked like cats and smacked their lips, giggling.

BACK HOME IN NEW MEXICO

MEZZA LUNA

I feel awake and so present this morning. Every breath I take is pleasure and aliveness.

Spring Again

oil

As the sun comes up behind the ridge, a half-moon still stands over the skylight above my bed. My body tingles with the joy of being home. Birdsong, I watch the fish in the pond chase each other. The bees are back, and so am I. What I feel is extraordinary. It is the same feeling I experience when I am in Bali or Florence. Everything, even the most familiar, can be new and special. How easy it is not to notice the rubies and diamonds in a familiar environment. It can be like this every day no matter where we are.

WINTER ON THE PECOS

I see seven skies today

sacred number sacred place

all is grey the sky melts into the land

blue sky is always there

mist roles down from the mesa

blue sky is there

it snows and hails

blue sky is there

mud splashes onto the roof of my car

blue sky is there

rainbow reaches across the valley

blue sky is there again

know it—reach for it—says the voice out of the tree.

Dec 21

WINTER SOLSTICE

I feel lonely today after coming home from town where I saw people in a festive Christmas mood, families and friends, children with parents, mothers and daughters. My own loss comes up. I am choking with grief. I feel some regret for choices I have made. I am looking in through the window again, an outsider seeing the table set while I have my feast with the birds. A cloud of blue jays swoops in like a group of Hell's Angels riding through town, falling in, feasting, the little birdhouse is covered with birds

Bring in the light; darkness is the absence of light. The light slowly comes back to shorten the long, dark nights again. I will greet the change tomorrow and make some offerings by the river with a fire—sage, cornmeal, tobacco, maybe drumming.

BE STILL

Cold winter sun—the night is bright with snow

frozen river black water moving under the ice makes me shiver

I make a fire on the bank to greet the rising sun

as I bring light into the darkness my heart sings with the wind:

river will run fast again before you know

first butterfly will wake from sleep

be still dear heart be still

river will run high again before you know

wind howling

blowing prisms of snow catching the light

flying diamonds in the sky

the prism in my window is casting rainbows on the wall

FIRST BUTTERFLY

Apricot blossoms framed in cerulean sky blue

I sit in the warm sun for a while

till my heart is in the right place

where is that place again?

RIVER RUN

Early beauty of the day

the sun warms my heart

I pull some weeds

make a fire

smoke signals to whom it may concern

the painting calls for blue green yellow

music makes my brush dance

my feet firm on the ground

no thought just letting go

the beauty of the day air wind new growth on the canvas

a miracle

no thought of tomorrow no words in my head

my fingers type I do not know what comes

in the studio maybe something will come

a dream please

the encaustic medium

I get something and then it is gone again

I work for it and cannot dance

I let go

then it happens

when I try too hard it is elusive

P O P P I E S

Red—against all caution

they popped their little caps off this morning

petals bright red not to be overlooked

against the pink wall

proud they stand

with hooded black eyes

they glance over to the yellow iris

on the other side of the pond

flirtatious waving back and fro in the wind

come over here they say

come be with me

I have wings to fly says Iris

but I'm firmly rooted in this ground

I love my home

bees come and go

birds drink from the pond

where do they go

is there another world I do not know about?

I greet you across the garden

that is as far as I can go

MOTHER

February 2010

This morning, grey and still

I am full of longing

a desire to be held

to feel a pulsing heart

other than my own

a little black cat outside

Is thankful for the food I put out

trusts my caressing hands

but will not sit on my lap

Blackfoot does not like this at all

in protest he withdraws his love from me

but not his watchful gaze.

This morning my mother called

a long-distance call what to do

exhausted from her effort to put herself to bed

across the ocean

my tears flow what can I do to help

she is withdrawing going to another place

I fear her leaving

S E H N S U C H T

Last night in my dream

answering my call

a gentle spirit touched me

eternal love tangible on my skin

flooding my heart

there next to me is another me

thin emaciated

held up toward the sky by spirit

I am crying shaking with emotion

I wake

eternal love stays with me all-day

the Other was my mother

BLACK BUTTERFLY

A long time ago

black butterflies flew away from me

to free my heart

a letter—burned paper—fluttered to the sky

leaving me behind to heal and find my way

I feel the wings I have grown

one black butterfly flew away from me again today

SUMMER SOLSTICE 2010

This day my mother passed into the light

last night she called

we laughed because we both had oatmeal for dinner

she said Auf Wiedersehn

her last words to me

she knew—

she passed in the morning.

GOLD OVER BLUE

A door opened

heart—breaking into the wind

thousand pieces flying to the stars

seeking joy in a million places

gold upon blue

circle of wisdom

mind not knowing

body still

heartbeat expanding to the universe

one for this moment

gold upon blue

a touch of wings

I laid my mother to rest in the earth

with lavender and summer jasmine

remembering the love she was

she will always be with me

here and now whenever I call her

weeping at her grave a bee came to me

sent to fly in circles in front of my face

now life has me back

my world here is overgrown

with sugar peas lamb's ear and daisies

dwarfing my humble existence

witnesses to the eternal cycle

joyfully reaching for the sky

B A R E F O O T   I N   T H E   G R A S S

Half-moon laughing on its side

river runs high

hummingbirds dance

smell the roses

listen to the raindrops on the roof

I get up early

the valley is new and fresh

from last night's rain

it feels good to be alive

Mutti you are everywhere

Pond VI

pastel

ALL KINDS OF LOVE

Four in the morning don't go back to sleep

in the darkness of the night

I was looking at the stars outside my window

then I saw a blue light

just standing in the corner of my room

a presence dark luminescent blue

just standing there

I imagined it was my angel

watching over me in the dark

not holding my hand

or telling me what to do

just stands there

soothing my soul

ARRIVAL TODAY

Hummingbirds

I hear their thrills in the air

but cannot see them

they sound happy and excited to be here

nothing yet to feed on

just air and my joy

I rush into the kitchen

And prepare a feeder with sugar water

in case my joy would not be enough

Love Medicine

pastel

Fierce Grace

It is snowing. New growth is covered with snowflakes—snowflakes so beautiful and miraculous. I can see beauty when I have no other expectations, desires or hope. Then I can accept what is presented to me, but I am ready for spring. My fruit trees have tried for the third time to put out buds, a promise of abundance and beauty. Nature, unwilling to give in to fear, comes forth with courage and faith. Today I am lacking both. The snowflakes cover this moment of crisis: I find human love and relationship very tenuous and conditional. I remind myself: the unconditional love I am seeking for myself I am often not willing to give.

The cycle of life and death

spring and winter

nature turns on herself as humans do

destruction and creation—grace

can I go through the heartbreak?

Let the light come in through the wound

I turn to my paintings and see the light

Fierce Grace

oil

God help me, be with me, show me the way. There is a rose waiting for me to smell. I am restless all day, remind myself to be still. It is then I feel the angel standing behind me—right behind me—folding me into his wings. Two wings cradling me. I put my head back on his shoulders. Be still. Be still.

S H A D O W

I woke up with a heavy heart

a shadow passing over my soul

I would think the wind could blow the cloud away

but instead my nerves are shaky

listen to the wind and the snow

drip from the roof

I am fighting what could be a soothing sound

instead of gratitude I feel loneliness

isolation weighs heavy on me today

If I go away—drive to tow run around aimlessly—

I will feel worse

be grateful to sit still

SNOW

Branches covered

bending under the weight

sun behind silver clouds

birds flock around the feeder

some peck on my window

thank you for feeding us

we will sing for you in the summer

God willing there will be a hand to feed me

a hand to touch me

a heart to love me

stillness outside

I go to get firewood

fetch water

for the love of God.

SOLITUDE

When I am stuck in a situation, when I have painted myself into a corner, when I don't know what comes next, suddenly something happens. And there, things are flowing again. Water bears no scars, going around obstacles. This is wisdom I want to live up to, climb that mountain

Living alone for many years is difficult at times. I work with intention, creating this space, inside and out, whispering to myself, inviting the devas to come to live here with me in the shadow of the trees. I create my reality with my thoughts and actions.

Be careful, be thoughtful about who you invite into your space—your physical energetic space and your heart space; be mindful about how much you give of yourself without losing your center. Focus on the invisible; there is so much to see. Make visible the invisible.

With brush and paint, pen and paper

I touch the blue

the circle closes—almost

Looking for the Mountain

pastel

BRIGITTE BRÜGGEMANN | 163

Printed in the United States
by Baker & Taylor Publisher Services